CONTENTS

**New Directions for
Teaching and Learning**

Catherine M. Wehlburg
Editor-in-Chief

Active Learning Spaces

Paul Baepler
D. Christopher Brooks
J. D. Walker

Editors

Number 137 • Spring 2014
Jossey-Bass
San Francisco

ACTIVE LEARNING SPACES
Paul Baepler, D. Christopher Brooks, J. D. Walker (eds.)
New Directions for Teaching and Learning, no. 137
Catherine M. Wehlburg, Editor-in-Chief

Copyright © 2014 Wiley Periodicals, Inc., A Wiley Company. All rights reserved. No part of this publication may be reproduced, stored in a retrieval system, or transmitted in any form or by any means, electronic, mechanical, photocopying, recording, scanning, or otherwise, except as permitted under Section 107 or 108 of the 1976 United States Copyright Act, without either the prior written permission of the Publisher or authorization through payment of the appropriate per-copy fee to the Copyright Clearance Center, 222 Rosewood Drive, Danvers, MA 01923, (978) 750-8400, fax (978) 646-8600. Requests to the Publisher for permission should be addressed to the Permissions Department, c/o John Wiley & Sons, Inc., 111 River St., Hoboken, NJ 07030; (201) 748-8789, fax (201) 748-6326, http://www.wiley.com/go/permissions.

Microfilm copies of issues and articles are available in 16 mm and 35 mm, as well as microfiche in 105 mm, through University Microfilms, Inc., 300 North Zeeb Road, Ann Arbor, MI 48106-1346.

NEW DIRECTIONS FOR TEACHING AND LEARNING (ISSN 0271-0633, electronic ISSN 1536-0768) is part of The Jossey-Bass Higher and Adult Education Series and is published quarterly by Wiley Subscription Services, Inc., A Wiley Company, at Jossey-Bass, One Montgomery Street, Suite 1200, San Francisco, CA 94104-4594. POSTMASTER: Send address changes to New Directions for Teaching and Learning, Jossey-Bass, One Montgomery Street, Suite 1200, San Francisco, CA 94104-4594.

New Directions for Teaching and Learning is indexed in CIJE: Current Index to Journals in Education (ERIC), Contents Pages in Education (T&F), Educational Research Abstracts Online (T&F), ERIC Database (Education Resources Information Center), Higher Education Abstracts (Claremont Graduate University), and SCOPUS (Elsevier).

INDIVIDUAL SUBSCRIPTION RATE (in USD): $89 per year US/Can/Mex, $113 rest of world; institutional subscription rate: $311 US, $351 Can/Mex, $385 rest of world. Single copy rate: $29. Electronic only–all regions: $89 individual, $311 institutional; Print & Electronic–US: $98 individual, $357 institutional; Print & Electronic–Can/Mex: $98 individual, $397 institutional; Print & Electronic–rest of world: $122 individual, $431 institutional.

EDITORIAL CORRESPONDENCE should be sent to the editor-in-chief, Catherine M. Wehlburg, c.wehlburg@tcu.edu.

www.josseybass.com

FROM THE SERIES EDITOR

About This Publication

Since 1980, *New Directions for Teaching and Learning* (NDTL) has brought a unique blend of theory, research, and practice to leaders in postsecondary education. NDTL sourcebooks strive not only for solid substance but also for timeliness, compactness, and accessibility.

The series has four goals: to inform readers about current and future directions in teaching and learning in postsecondary education, to illuminate the context that shapes these new directions, to illustrate these new direction through examples from real settings, and to propose ways in which these new directions can be incorporated into still other settings.

This publication reflects the view that teaching deserves respect as a high form of scholarship. We believe that significant scholarship is conducted not only by researchers who report results of empirical investigations but also by practitioners who share disciplinary reflections about teaching. Contributors to NDTL approach questions of teaching and learning as seriously as they approach substantive questions in their own disciplines, and they deal not only with pedagogical issues but also with the intellectual and social context in which these issues arise. Authors deal on the one hand with theory and research and on the other with practice, and they translate from research and theory to practice and back again.

About This Volume

This volume of *New Directions for Teaching and Learning* explores the history, research, and the related teaching practices to active learning spaces. Active learning spaces are redesigned spaces in which students learn that are often hybrids of traditional classroom space that is enhanced with technology, new flexible arrangements, and even laboratory options. Traditionally designed rooms often do not provide the options that a more flexible space that is necessary as we look at twenty-first century pedagogies and technologies. As classroom space is redesigned, there are a myriad of educational implications for this new engineered space. This volume addresses these issues and provides examples of active learning spaces that allow for enhanced learning.

Catherine Wehlburg
Editor-in-Chief

EDITORS' NOTES

Over the last two decades, colleges and universities have devoted substantial resources to the construction and reconfiguration of learning spaces. This movement began in the 1990s with North Carolina State University's Student-Centered Activities for Large Enrollment Undergraduate Programs (SCALE-UP) project, which sought to reform the teaching of large introductory physics courses by reworking the layout and technology of the classrooms in which those courses were taught. The new learning spaces contained round tables for student seating, laptop connectivity, and easy access to lab equipment (Beichner et al. 2007).

Somewhat later, MIT began the Technology Enabled Active Learning (TEAL) project, which was modeled on SCALE-UP in the sense that it was designed to transform both the pedagogy and learning spaces associated with a physics course, but it differed in that the targeted course relied heavily on computer-based simulations and visualizations and focused class time on student-centered, collaborative learning activities (Dori and Belcher 2005). Following the SCALE-UP and TEAL projects, a number of universities began new construction or refitting of learning spaces along similar lines, including the TILE initiative at the University of Iowa, Wallenberg Hall's experimental classrooms at Stanford University, and the creation of active learning classrooms (ALCs) at the University of Minnesota. In 2009, Minnesota increased its inventory of ALCs to 17, and by 2013, over 36 percent of all undergraduates had taken a course in one. The large-scale adoption of these new classrooms at Minnesota fundamentally changed the idea of what a common classroom might look like at a large institution (see Figures 1 and 2).

In recent years, the field of educational technology has built on these pioneering projects by attempting to understand learning spaces themselves and the relationship of those spaces to teaching and learning in higher education. EDUCAUSE, a leading American organization created to promote and evaluate technological advances in higher education, has been at the forefront of this movement by devoting entire issues of their flagship publications to the subject, producing a number of reports from administrators, technologists, and instructors, and publishing a book length treatment of the subject (Oblinger 2006). So widespread has the interest in new learning spaces been that a new journal, the *Journal of Learning Spaces*, has been founded to address specific issues related to this new phenomenon. Despite the enthusiasm expressed for transforming formal learning spaces, there is a paucity of systematic research examining the effects of these environments on teaching practices and student learning.

NEW DIRECTIONS FOR TEACHING AND LEARNING, no. 137, Spring 2014 © 2014 Wiley Periodicals, Inc.
Published online in Wiley Online Library (wileyonlinelibrary.com) • DOI: 10.1002/tl.20080

Figure 1. One of the Early ALCs at the University of Minnesota

Figure 2. A More Recent ALC at the University of Minnesota, in the Science Teaching and Student Services Building

Literature Review

The movement to reconsider formal learning spaces on college and university campuses appears to be predicated upon a set of assumptions regarding the potential influence of physical space on student-learning experiences and outcomes. While researchers, practitioners, and instructors have repeated these assumptions in a variety of ways and contexts, Amedeo, Golledge, and Stimson's (2009) methodological consideration of the relation of space to human behavior articulates them summarily in three statements. The first assumption is that space, while not directly causal, "exerts significant influences on [human activity and experience] through complex and intricate relationships" (12). Stated more simply, a space does not *determine* behavior, but *influences* how we act and relate within it in ways that may not be readily observable. Second, the meaning of spaces depends primarily on "translations of [the] properties [of the space] by individuals

NEW DIRECTIONS FOR TEACHING AND LEARNING • DOI: 10.1002/tl.20080 engaged in processing context information in which those properties are an inextricable part" (12). In other words, how a space is used determines how individuals relate to and experience it. Finally, the meaning of a space is "affected by two fundamental and generic features of space: its structuring and its scaling effects" (13). That is, the physical layout and scale of a space constrains and/or facilitates the manner in which individuals relate to or experience a space.

Until recently, however, none of these assumptions have been subjected to empirical testing in the field of learning spaces research. Instead, three approaches to the discussion of the relationship of formal learning spaces to student learning have dominated the landscape. One of these veins of scholarship has focused on the architectural features of learning space design by either showcasing particular innovative approaches or musing about the latent potential for instructional innovation inherent to new designs (Lippincott 2009; Long and Holeton 2009; Oblinger 2006). Another vein can be characterized by normative, theoretical, and practical assertions about the importance of learning spaces that offer little to no empirical evidence in support of the claims (Boddington and Boys 2011; Savin-Baden 2008; Summerfield and Smith 2011; Thomas 2010). The last area of learning spaces research devotes considerable attention to pedagogical issues related to teaching in such spaces. They include such things as case studies, lessons learned, best practices, and practical recommendations, few of which are subjected to rigorous empirical testing (Jankowska and Atlay 2008; Jorn, Whiteside, and Duin 2009; Montgomery 2008).

While the call for empirical research that evaluates the efficacy and impact of formal learning spaces on student learning has proliferated (Bligh and Pearshouse 2011; Hunley and Schaller 2009; Savin-Baden, McFarland, and Savin-Baden 2008; Temple 2008), most of the work in this area has focused on data related to feedback on experiences within new spaces or measures of satisfaction from student and faculty users (Jankowska and Atlay 2008; Matthews, Andrews, and Adams 2011; Soderdahl 2011). There are two important exceptions to these more impressionistic lines of inquiry in which researchers attempted to empirically demonstrate the impact of technologically enhanced formal learning spaces on student-learning outcomes. The first of these was conducted by Massachusetts Institute of Technology researchers who in assessing their TEAL project found that the newly designed spaces and curriculum designed for them contributed to higher rates of conceptual understanding and lower rates of failure than traditional classrooms with lecture-based approaches (Dori et al. 2003). North Carolina State University researchers are responsible for the other project that was conducted as part of their assessment of the SCALE-UP initiative. Similar to the results of the TEAL project, Robert Beichner and his colleagues (2007) found that the SCALE-UP classrooms and curriculum reduced failure rates, improved levels of conceptual understanding, and improved problem-solving skills, class attendance rates, and attitudes of students enrolled in its courses. Despite their pioneering empirical contributions to the field of learning spaces research, the lack of rigorous controls on their research designs and the potential conflation of the impact of space and course redesign as explanations for differences in outcomes limit their ability to isolate the impact of formal learning spaces on student behavior and learning outcomes.

The quasi-experimental designs we have employed at the University of Minnesota to assess the impact of our ALCs have afforded us a host of controls that greatly enhance our ability to test the theoretical assumptions mentioned earlier. We were able to test the first assumption—that space is indirectly causal—using a within term quasi-experimental design in which *all* aspects of an introductory biology course were held constant, including the instructor, materials, assignments, schedules, exams, and time of day. Despite a lack of randomization of student participants, equivalency was established between student groups with the exception of their college entry, composite ACT scores. The only factor that we allowed to vary systematically was the type of classroom in which the course was held: the section in which students happened to have higher test scores met in a traditional classroom while the section with students who were found to have lower test scores met in the ALC. Because ACT scores are good predictors of student grades in introductory courses like the one in this study, and because the traditional-room students had significantly higher ACT scores than the students in the ALC, we would expect a gap in achievement favoring the students in the traditional room. This gap, however, was not found in mean student final grades, indicating that the expected disparity in achievement based on test scores was statistically erased. Given the quasi-experimental controls used in the study, the results clearly demonstrated that space has an independent and significant impact on student learning, as measured by grades (Brooks 2011).

While supporting the first assumption about spatial causality, there are likely more proximate factors leading to the accelerated pace of learning experienced by students in the ALC compared to their traditional classroom counterparts. We think at least two sets of mechanisms are at work in giving the ALCs an edge in producing the observed results: (1) effects of the new learning spaces on student classroom experiences and (2) the instructional behavior and classroom activities. On the first point, students whose section met in the ALC were significantly more likely than students meeting in the traditional classroom to think that the space enriched their learning experience, afforded them a more flexible learning experience, engaged them in the learning process, and fit the course being taught there (Walker, Brooks, and Baepler 2011; Whiteside, Brooks, and Walker 2010).

On the second mechanism, despite the instructor's best efforts to teach each section of the course identically, our classroom observation data reveal that the different rooms engendered significantly different behaviors and activities. For example, the instructor remained at the podium and lectured significantly more in the traditional classroom than in the ALC. Conversely, he consulted with students and led classroom discussion significantly more frequently in the ALC than in traditional classroom (Brooks 2012). We were able to conclude that the particular characteristics embodied by the traditional classroom led to the instructor lecturing significantly more, which, in turn, led to on-task student behavior while the features and layout of the ALC led to the instructor using group activities and classroom discussion to get students to perform (Whiteside, Brooks, and Walker 2010). Stated more simply, different spaces led to different forms of instructional behavior and classroom activities that subsequently elicited the contextually appropriate student behaviors. When coupled with the evidence that students in the ALC closed an expected achievement gap, these results provide considerable evidence in support of Amedeo, Golledge, and Stimson's (2009) third assumption that "space exerts situation-related influences on human activities and experiences as they are enacted and felt in [specific] environmental settings" (13).

Our research on the impact of formal learning spaces has produced evidence in support of the second theoretical assumption about the relationship of physical space to human activities as well. That assumption suggests that a space exerts its influence through individuals and the ways in which they use that space, and that some approaches to using a space in service of a particular goal are better at accomplishing that task than others. It is important to test this hypothesis because one possible reaction to the results described above is to think that new classroom spaces exert such a strong influence on the learning process that there is no need for instructors to modify classes taught in such classrooms; that is, the space by itself will do all the work.

In 2008–2009, we used a between-semesters quasi-experimental research design to test this hypothesis. In this study (which is described in much greater detail in Chapter 5), a single instructor taught the same course in the same ALC twice, in fall 2008 and fall 2009. The main factor that varied between the two semesters was the instructor's approach to teaching: the first iteration of the class was largely lecture based, while the second iteration was redesigned with student-centered pedagogy in mind and incorporated numerous team-based learning activities.

We found two significant differences in outcomes between the two classes compared in this study. First, we noted that student reactions to the classroom in which both classes were taught were statistically identical across the two semesters, with one exception: students in the redesigned fall 2009 class agreed much more strongly that their classroom encouraged their active participation. And second, we found that the fall 2009 students significantly outperformed the fall 2008 students in terms of final grades in the class. In this instance, when the instructor changed her teaching practice from a lecture-based approach to a team-based design, students performed better on all categories of assessments than their counterparts in the same classroom a year before.

Given the controls in place in this study along with the demographic equivalence of the students in the two semesters, our results support Amedeo, Golledge, and Stimson's (2009) second assumption by showing that using a learning space in different ways produces different experiences on the part of learners and, possibly as a consequence, yields different educational outcomes. The practical application of this finding suggests that targeted faculty development—the subject of several chapters in this volume—may improve learning and student experiences.

These recent empirical studies have begun to set a foundation for future work, including some of the chapters you'll read in this volume of *New Directions for Teaching and Learning*. This collection was designed to include empirical research, practical reflection, and historical perspectives on learning spaces. We bring forward this volume to consolidate much of the current thinking on active learning spaces and to acknowledge the advancement of such an important topic about physical space at a moment in time when virtual and online spaces are grabbing headlines. In large measure, how we configure our new brick and mortar classrooms will set the agenda for how face-to-face teaching continues to change and transform student learning. Indeed, active learning classrooms have become an integral component of the argument in favor of face-to-face learning experiences, placing students in environments that take greater advantage of peer and instructor interaction and making innovative pedagogies such as team-based and problem-based learning easier to enact. We hope this volume serves as a basis to continue the conversation about the value of these rooms that began with the first SCALE-UP classrooms several decades ago and that it points to new directions for research on their place in higher education.

Acknowledgments

The editors would like to thank the following individuals who contributed their time, encouragement, insights, and resources to this volume and to the greater project of understanding active learning spaces. Our faculty partners, Sehoya Cotner, Chris Cramer, Mark Decker, Jigna Desai, Michelle Driessen, Jay Hatch, David Matthes, Tom Molitor, Leslie Schiff, Catherine Solheim, Sue Wick, Robin Wright. Senior Vice President for Academic Affairs and Provost, Karen Hanson, and Vice Provost and Dean of Undergraduate Education, Robert McMaster. Director of the Office of Classroom Management, Jeremy Todd. Director of the Office of Institutional Research, John Kellogg, as well as the Associate Director, Ron Huesman. Associate CIO of Academic Technology in the Office of Information Technology, Bradley A. Cohen. And Associate Vice Provost of Learning Technologies and Division of Information Technology (DoIT) Director of Academic Technology, at the University of Wisconsin Madison, Linda Jorn.

D. Christopher Brooks
J. D. Walker
Paul Baepler
Editors

References

Amedeo, D., R. G. Golledge, and R. J. Stimson. 2009. *Person Environment Behavior Research: Investigating Activities and Experiences in Spaces and Environments*. New York, NY: Guilford.

Beichner, R., J. M. Saul, D. S. Abbott, J. J. Morse, D. L. Deardorff, and R. J. Allain. 2007. "Student-Centered Activities for Large Enrollment Undergraduate Programs (SCALE-UP) Project." In *Research-Based Reform of University Physics*, edited by E. Redish and P. Cooney, 1–42. College Park, MD: American Association of Physics Teachers.

Bligh, B., and I. Pearshouse. 2011. "Doing Learning Space Evaluations." In *Re-Shaping Learning: A Critical Reader. The Future of Learning Spaces in Post-Compulsory Education*, edited by A. Boddington and J. Boys, 3–18. Rotterdam, The Netherlands: Sense Publishers.

Boddington, A., and J. Boys. 2011. *Re-Shaping Learning: A Critical Reader. The Future of Learning Spaces in Post-Compulsory Education*. Rotterdam, The Netherlands: Sense Publishers.

Brooks, D. C. 2011. "Space Matters: The Impact of Formal Learning Environments on Student Learning." *British Journal of Educational Technology* 42 (5): 719–726.

Brooks, D. C. 2012. "Space and Consequences: The Impact of Different Formal Learning Spaces on Instructor and Student Behavior." *Journal of Learning Spaces* 1 (2). http://libjournal.uncg.edu/ojs/index.php/jls/article/view/285/275.

Dori, Y. J., and J. Belcher. 2005. "How Does Technology-Enabled Active Learning Affect Undergraduate Students' Understanding of Electromagnetism Concepts?" *The Journal of the Learning Sciences* 14: 243–279.

Dori, Y. J., J. Belcher, M. Besette, M. Danziger, A. McKinney, and E. Hult. 2003. "Technology for Active Learning." *Materials Today* 6: 44–49.

Hunley, S., and M. Schaller. 2009. "Assessment: The Key to Creating Spaces That Promote Learning." *EDUCAUSE Review* 44: 26–35.

Jankowska, M., and M. Atlay. 2008. "Use of Creative Space in Enhancing Students' Engagement." *Innovations in Education and Teaching International* 45 (3): 271–279.

Jorn, L., A. Whiteside, and A. H. Duin. 2009. "PAIR-up." *EDUCAUSE Review* 44: 12–15.

Lippincott, J. K. 2009. "Learning Spaces: Involving Faculty to Improve Pedagogy." *EDUCAUSE Review* 44: 16–25.

Long, P. D., and R. Holeton. 2009. "Signposts to a Revolution? What We Talk about when We Talk about Learning Spaces." *EDUCAUSE Review* 44: 36–48.

Matthews, K., V. Andrews, and P. Adams. 2011. "Social Learning Spaces and Student Engagement." *Higher Education Research & Development* 30 (2): 105–120.

Montgomery, T. 2008. "Space Matters: Experiences of Managing Static Formal Learning Spaces." *Active Learning in Higher Education* 9: 122–138.

Oblinger, D. G. 2006. *Learning Spaces*. Washington, DC: EDUCAUSE.

Savin-Baden, M. 2008. *Learning Spaces: Creating Opportunities for Knowledge Creation in Academic Life*. New York, NY: Open University.

Savin-Baden, M., L. McFarland, and J. Savin-Baden. 2008. "Learning Spaces, Agency and Notions of Improvement: What Influences Thinking and Practices about Teaching and Learning in Higher Education? An Interpretive Meta-Ethnography." *London Review of Education* 6 (3): 211–227.

Soderdahl, P. A. 2011. "Library Classroom Renovated as an Active Learning Classroom." *Library Hi Tech* 29 (1): 83–90.

Summerfield, J., and C. C. Smith, eds. 2011. *Making Teaching and Learning Matter: Transformative Spaces in Higher Education.* Explorations of Educational Purpose, vol. 11. New York, NY: Springer. doi:10.1007/978-90-481-9166-6.

Temple, P. 2008. "Learning Spaces in Higher Education: An Under-Researched Topic." *London Review of Education* 6 (3): 229–241.

Thomas, H. 2010. "Learning Spaces, Learning Environments and the Dis'placement' of Learning." *British Journal of Educational Technology* 41 (3): 502–511.

Walker, J. D., D. C. Brooks, and P. Baepler. 2011. "Pedagogy and Space: Empirical Research on New Learning Environments." *EDUCAUSE Quarterly* 34 (4). http://z.umn.edu/eq1.

Whiteside, A., D. C. Brooks, and J. D. Walker. 2010. "Making the Case for Space: Three Years of Empirical Research on Learning Environments." *EDUCAUSE Quarterly* 33 (3). http://z.umn.edu/22m.

D. CHRISTOPHER BROOKS *is a senior research fellow for the Data, Research, and Analytics team at EDUCAUSE, where he conducts research on the impact of educational technologies in higher education.*

J. D. WALKER *is part of the research and evaluation team in Information Technology at the University of Minnesota.*

PAUL BAEPLER *is part of the research and evaluation team in Information Technology at the University of Minnesota.*

1

This chapter examines active learning spaces as they have developed over the years. Consistently well-designed classrooms can facilitate active learning even though the details of implementing pedagogies may differ.

History and Evolution of Active Learning Spaces

Robert J. Beichner

The value and efficacy of active learning is discussed in detail elsewhere in this volume. In this chapter, we focus our attention on the origins of classrooms designed to facilitate active learning.

Why Should Learning Spaces Change?

Before we describe the commonalities and differences of active learning environments, we should first consider why we would want to make these modifications from our "tried and true" classrooms in the first place. Some of the classroom adaptations can be quite expensive, so we should have a good reason to go down this path of educational reform.

The World Is Different.   Our species has changed from hunter-gatherers to fast-food fanatics. In fact, the current overabundance of food has resulted in serious health problems as our bodies continue to seek calorie-rich satiation. This would have been absolutely unthinkable a dozen generations ago, just yesterday in our evolutionary history. In an analogous manner, we've gone from carefully copied manuscripts owned by an elite few to online blogs published by teenagers. Our legal system and ideas of morality have yet to catch up, as copyright laws are ignored and "sexting" is practiced by a sizable fraction of our youth. Today's students are used to and expect continuous connection to information and people. Forcing them to put their personal technology away during class contradicts the way they live their lives and gives students one more reason to expect that what they learn in school will have little relationship to reality.

Information Is Readily Accessible.   A Google search on the word "google" results in 12 billion hits in less than 1/100th of a second.

NEW DIRECTIONS FOR TEACHING AND LEARNING, no. 137, Spring 2014 © 2014 Wiley Periodicals, Inc.
Published online in Wiley Online Library (wileyonlinelibrary.com) • DOI: 10.1002/tl.20081

Additionally, the list of relevant websites it produces is not in random, alphabetical, or even chronological order. Google's amazing search algorithms somehow sort the results so well that if you can't find what you are looking for on the first or second page of hits, you probably need to tweak your search terms. The advent of tablets and smartphones has put the world's published information literally at our fingertips. Today's students have grown up with ubiquitous access to a storehouse more vast than the Library of Congress, and it's much more densely indexed! Shouldn't that change what happens in schools?

Students Are Different.   Today's college students probably learned to read by using Google, so they are very familiar with technology and have grown accustomed to and expect instantaneous feedback. This affects student attitudes toward academic authority. Why should a student think of their professor as their only source of knowledge when their phone, in a fraction of a second, can find content that is more up to date than today's lecture? And what if the instructor is trying to promulgate some suspect scheme like evolution? A quick search of the web produces scores of beautifully designed sites that convincingly explain that evolution is "just a theory." Faculty no longer hold the monopoly on sources of information.

Technology has literally changed the way students think. People are often better at remembering how to find information than recalling the information itself. In a very real sense, our cognition is evolving. Evolution is the changing of some aspect of an organism because of a change in its environment. In this case, information is everywhere so we don't need to remember all the facts, just how to locate them. It only makes sense that our brains, a part of the body that was designed to very rapidly modify itself in response to internal or external stimulus (which is all that learning is), would display this type of evolutionary change.

Nowadays, people use technology from a very young age. 75 percent of children under age four use computers. The typical 8- to 18-year-old spends seven and a half hours per day watching a screen, viewing nearly 11 hours of content. They average an outgoing text message every five minutes. We used to worry that watching too much TV would shorten kids' attention spans. That has probably happened, but today's technology has caused students to expect instant feedback and gratification when seeking something, be it information or contact with a friend. Although they might be willing to sit quietly and watch a movie (probably on a personal device rather than a television or cinema screen), it is more likely that they will also have a chat screen open as well as Facebook or Twitter. When they see a familiar actress, they might use IMDB to find out what other films she has made. They repeatedly reach out and fetch anything that is of interest to them at that moment. The world of information revolves around them. This has made it harder for students to learn from the kind of patient, orderly presentation that their teachers prefer. We have to do something different to reach

NEW DIRECTIONS FOR TEACHING AND LEARNING • DOI: 10.1002/tl

them. We need to change classrooms so that students don't have to just sit passively, but can actively participate in their learning.

So Why Are Lecture Halls So Common?

There is an easy answer to why we've kept using lecture halls for so many years...they worked for us! But we in academia are quite unlike most of our students.

Formal classrooms have a long history. There were instructional spaces in ancient Samaria that were clearly teacher-centric. To uncover the history of lecture halls we have to take a sidetrack. One of the earliest large-scale spaces where many people watched an individual or small band of performers was the Theatre of Dionysus in Athens. It dates from about 500 BCE. Dionysus was the Greek god of wine and the space was used for religious services. It was also an entertainment venue for the plays that were popular 2500 years ago. Our word "theatre" comes from the Greek word for the "beholding area" where patrons would sit to view the spectacle. A few generations later the Romans had similar uses for their spaces, which they called "auditoria" and filled with the "audience." Evidently instead of "beholding" like the Greeks, the Romans were listening to the audio aspects of the events being presented! All was good and these spaces served their intended purposes very well.

About 1000 years later, Pope Gregory VII decided the clergy needed to be educated. This was a good idea since clerics were very powerful and it was important that they all were properly trained in Church dogma. As far as I can ascertain, this was the first time in history that a large number of people needed to be educated at once. Up until then, teachers worked with their small, loyal band of disciples. Now the economics of scale required a new approach and the Pope came up with a brilliant solution. The clergy often lived in monasteries that had auditoria for their religious services. Many of these monks were unbelievably good at copying things down. People would spend their entire adult lives copying scriptures with incredible accuracy. Gregory's clever idea was to use the existing technology to capitalize on and extend people's skills. The auditoria were filled with monks sitting in what now became lecture halls, copying down the words read by the "lecturer" (from the Latin for "reader") as they progressed through their manuscript. Lecturers could actually be fined if they deviated from what was written in front of them. When finished, each clergyman had their very own faithfully copied manuscript and they could hire themselves out as a lecturer somewhere else. Considering that the Pope's decree came down in 1079, nearly 400 years before Gutenberg's printing press, this was a fantastic way to accurately duplicate and disseminate materials. In fact, it was such a great combination of ideas that we've been continuing to do it for more than ten centuries.

NEW DIRECTIONS FOR TEACHING AND LEARNING • DOI: 10.1002/tl

Change Arrives Slowly

Lecturing is really a logical continuation of very ancient oral traditions of religious and cultural education, which sprang from times when reading and writing skills were very rare or even nonexistent. As more and more people sought education, an industry arose to meet society's needs. Early universities in Bologna, Paris, and elsewhere perpetuated the lecture model, even after the advent of the printing press. Requiring students to attend lectures, when they could have independently read the material in one of the rapidly growing number of books, allowed teachers to maintain their historically authoritative role.

Active Learning in Labs.   For the most part, this was the story until we finally reach modern times. By then, teachers had noticed that their students were not learning as much as they should from the lecture approach. European chemists like Friedrich Stromyer and Johann von Fuchs began supplementing their lectures with laboratory work in the early 1800s. The first American to do this (in engineering) is believed to be Amos Eaton, who cofounded the Rensselaer Institute of Technology in 1824. In 1906 Robert Millikan, the physicist most well-known for finding the charge on a single electron, wrote a popular lab manual where he advocated the importance of hands-on experience to help students learn difficult concepts. He suggested what has since become a standard approach, which is to supplement three hours of lecture per week with two hours for laboratory. So teachers, at least in the sciences, were beginning to relinquish the position of the lecture as the sole means of instruction and incorporate active learning as part of their students' education.

By the 1980s, nearly all science programs were aware of anecdotal evidence that students benefitted from hands-on activities and so most offered lecture/lab combination courses. The idea of learning from interesting tasks had also spread to other content areas like foreign languages. Of course, performance-based classes in areas like music and the arts had existed for millennia. No one expected to learn how to play an oboe by just listening to someone tell them how to do it. Also during this time medical schools, starting with McMasters University, began trying what is now called problem-based learning or PBL. Students practiced hypothetical-deductive reasoning by solving complex, often real, medical cases. This approach, now accepted as standard practice for medical education, has since been applied to instruction across all scientific areas, although not as widely as the lecture/lab combination.

During the 1990s, a growing body of rigorous research on learning began providing irrefutable data illustrating that students in lecture settings simply did not learn as much as their teachers hoped. The famous Force Concept Inventory in physics led the way with Richard Hake and others supplying embarrassingly consistent indicators of students' poor grasp of conceptual knowledge when they were taught in passive lecture settings.

Perhaps recognizing the futility of trying to change lecture-based instruction, or maybe realizing that greater gains could be made by improving laboratory experiences, a large group of creative people began building and testing new instructional technologies for the lab. Ron Thornton and David Sokoloff designed a series of sensors and accompanying software for what came to be called microcomputer-based labs or MBLs. These became extremely popular and essentially revolutionized what could be done in a laboratory setting. This required institutions to provide space and electrical power for computers, eventually setting up network connections as well. Many studies showed that MBLs and their offspring, video-based labs, helped students learn considerably more than when sitting and listening to straight lecturing.

Active Learning in Lectures.   Faculty were still enamored with the lecture method, so people found ways to incorporate the newly developed technology into their classes, essentially making it less likely that students would simply sit and passively listen. Probably the most sophisticated approach is the interactive lecture demo (ILD) which has students in a lecture hall or a classroom (but not a lab) watch a demonstration and then predict the kind of data that would soon be gathered from teacher-operated computer sensors. Studies have shown considerable learning gains when instructors carefully follow the detailed ILD instructions.

One of the most popular uses of technology in lecture halls is the student response system or "clickers." (These have actually been around for quite some time. Cornell's Raphael Littauer used wired systems to collect student responses in the early 1970s.) This approach was greatly popularized by Eric Mazur at Harvard, who developed a technique he called Peer Instruction. Students are asked a carefully crafted question designed to elicit misunderstandings. They think for a minute and press a button on a remote control-like device to indicate their answer. The instructor displays a bar chart of the results, which often indicate a substantial difference of opinion across the class. Students are then encouraged to talk to their peers for a minute or two and revote. The updated bar chart shows that usually the logic of the correct answer wins the debate. This type of instruction promotes very active discussion, even in large lecture halls. In addition to this obvious advantage, it also provides the instructor with immediate and often surprising feedback on how misunderstandings can persist even after students listen to their carefully crafted lectures.

Trying to couple lectures and laboratories is an important means of improving the educational experience of students. However, it can be difficult to keep the two types of class synchronized, especially if there are multiple sections of each. Students with lab scheduled on Mondays may not have seen the material before, so their hands-on activity requires a sort of "discovery" of the principles, based on observations. In other words, they would be applying inductive reasoning. Peers who don't take lab until later in the week might have already been exposed to the concepts in a Wednesday lecture. Their lab now becomes an exercise in verification and deductive reasoning. These two approaches are very different. Nonetheless, lecture/lab combinations, in the format suggested by Millikan in 1906, are still the norm.

History of Studios.   Over the past two decades, efforts have been made to combine lecture classes and lab experiences into a single learning experience. Original work along these lines has been done in several places and now the "studio approach" is spreading rapidly across hundreds of institutions.

Of course, studios are not new. They stem from medieval apprenticeships, where students worked closely with the master to actively learn some craft or art. Eventually this sort of approach found its way into places like the Ecole des Beaux Arts in Paris, where students were judged based on the quality of their architectural design projects. The Bauhaus School in Germany was well-known for its practical instruction in architecture, with students even working on construction sites.

Although starting in the arts and architecture, active learning eventually found its way into the general curriculum. The Quincy School System in Massachusetts had elementary students experiencing "constant activity" in the late 1800s, in what was called a "New Departure" from American education. Around the same time, John Dewey's Laboratory School in Chicago incorporated collaborative learning into learning studios for older students. A few years later, the Horace Mann High School in Gary, Indiana, followed up on Dewey's ideas and had students presenting to each other and critiquing everyone's work.

Active Learning in Studios.   A fairly recent advance is the use of studios for science, technology, math, and engineering (STEM) courses, where the studio structure makes it easy to move back and forth between teacher presentation and student experimentation or other activity. This eliminates the synchronization problem of separate lecture and lab sections and replaces much of the less effective lecture time with active learning.

Priscilla Laws and colleagues created Workshop Physics in the late 1980s and early 1990s at Dickinson College. She made full use of MBL and PBL technologies and was able to replace lectures entirely with activities. Many of the experiments done by Workshop students promote kinesthetic learning. Before long the approach spread to other content areas like chemistry and biology. The influence of the Workshop Physics approach can be seen in all of today's science studios.

One of the first (and few) places to adopt the studio approach on a school-wide basis was Rensselaer Polytechnic Institute (RPI). In the 1990s, under the leadership of Provost Jack Wilson, RPI converted many of their classrooms to studio designs. An assortment of high tech tools helped students as they worked. However, research found that implementing a studio space alone was not sufficient to ensure improvements in learning. This renovated classroom needed to be accompanied by research-based

NEW DIRECTIONS FOR TEACHING AND LEARNING • DOI: 10.1002/tl

Figure 1.1. SCALE-UP Classroom at NCSU, Seating Ninety-Nine Students

Note: Beichner suggests only one computer per team of three students. The room has one laptop per student since it is also used as a computer lab.
Source: Photo courtesy of Robert Beichner.

pedagogical techniques before significant gains on nationally normed tests were seen.

The first attempt to bring the benefits of collaborative, studio-based learning to larger classes was the SCALE-UP (Student-Centered Activities for Large Enrollment Undergraduate Programs) project at North Carolina State University in the mid-1990s. Figure 1.1 shows the typical set of round tables whose purpose is to facilitate interactions between students and with the roaming instructor. Earlier research by a team led by Alexander Astin found that the quality of relationships students have with others is highly correlated with their academic success. The SCALE-UP table design was specifically selected to enhance social networking. Whiteboards surround the room as public thinking spaces and supplement smaller, group-sized boards. Teams of three students work on interesting problems, take measurements or make observations, or write computer models of physical phenomena. Research has documented a wide variety of advantages, including a five-fold reduction in failure rates for female students. The approach has since spread so that its use is no longer confined to just physics courses, or even large classes. All STEM areas as well as art, language, humanities, literature, and so on, have been taught using this approach. Class sizes at more than two hundred adopting institutions range from 24 to 200. Because of SCALE-UP's expansion, project director Robert Beichner changed the acronym to mean Student-Centered Active Learning Environment with Upside-down Pedagogies. The name now includes both the redesigned instructional space and the reformed pedagogy used inside.

Future of Active Learning Classrooms

Classrooms that make it easier for students to actively participate in their learning are becoming more and more common. Spaces that are formally associated with just the SCALE-UP approach can be found at more than two hundred institutions. Although this particular room design originally featured round tables, smaller SCALE-UP classrooms often have students seated at smaller "D"-shaped tables located around the periphery of the studio. Thus, they end up looking very much like the Workshop Physics arrangements first created at Dickinson College. This is no coincidence. Successful active learning classrooms, regardless of how many students are in the space, are designed to facilitate interactions between students as they work collaboratively on interesting tasks. Spaces and the furnishings within them are carefully designed with features that enable students to meet the goals of instruction. These goals vary from course to course and institution, but they increasingly include twenty-first century skills like problem solving, communication, and teamsmanship. Active learning classrooms make it easy for faculty to assign tasks that require students to practice these skills as a means of learning the subject matter.

Evidence pointing out the efficacy of active learning continues to accumulate. At the same time, colleges and universities are feeling competitive pressure from online institutions and freely available course materials distributed via the web. The "flipped classroom," where most course content is delivered outside of a formal learning space, is gaining in popularity. These outside influences are leading faculty to ask themselves how they can best use the valuable but limited time they have in the classroom with their students. Because active learning spaces and the research-based pedagogies they enable provide a readily available and well-tested answer, they will have a growing impact on the instructional scene.

ROBERT J. BEICHNER *is an alumni distinguished undergraduate professor of physics at North Carolina State University. He directs the NCST STEM (Science, Technology, Engineering, and Math) Education Initiative.*

NEW DIRECTIONS FOR TEACHING AND LEARNING • DOI: 10.1002/tl

2

This chapter describes the results of an assessment project whose purpose was to improve the faculty-development program for instructors who teach in technology-infused TILE (Transform, Interact, Learn, Engage) classrooms at the University of Iowa. Qualitative research methods were critical for (1) learning about how students and instructors interacted in these new learning spaces and (2) improving faculty development to ensure that instructors could design and implement effective learning activities in the TILE environment.

Using Qualitative Research to Assess Teaching and Learning in Technology-Infused TILE Classrooms

Sam Van Horne, Cecilia Titiek Murniati, Kem Saichaie, Maggie Jesse, Jean C. Florman, Beth F. Ingram

Introduction

The vision for TILE (Transform, Interact, Learn, Engage) classrooms originated in the spring of 2009, just months after a flood devastated the University of Iowa (UI) campus and in the midst of the Great Recession. Either of these challenging events might have pushed campus leaders to entrench and turn to well-known, risk-averse instructional delivery methods in traditional classrooms. Instead, a group of campus leaders used these two challenges to lead a change effort with the potential to improve student recruitment, increase student retention, bolster student success, use limited spaces more creatively, and build enthusiasm for new teaching models across campus.

This ambitious project, modeled after the SCALE-UP classrooms at North Carolina State University, leveraged federal stimulus funding and campus spaces that had been freed up by the closing of discipline-specific libraries. Leaders encouraged broad campus involvement to create interactive, high-tech classrooms and adopted the TILE acronym to highlight the principles of these rooms which were created to transform teaching and learning through increased student-faculty interaction and engagement. TILE classrooms are administered as a collaborative effort between

New Directions for Teaching and Learning, no. 137, Spring 2014 © 2014 Wiley Periodicals, Inc.
Published online in Wiley Online Library (wileyonlinelibrary.com) • DOI: 10.1002/tl.20082

Figure 2.1. Picture of 81-Seat TILE Classroom

Source: Photograph by Mike Jenn.

ITS-Instructional Services and the Center for Teaching, who develop training for faculty about how to facilitate active learning in classrooms that are designed to facilitate computer-supported, collaborative learning.

The TILE classrooms consist of round tables that seat nine students each, projectors and wall-mounted monitors that facilitate the sharing of information, and glass whiteboards for working out longer problems (see Figure 2.1 for an image of the 81-seat TILE classroom). Similar to the SCALE-UP classrooms, these learning environments are particularly suited to supporting certain learning strategies that involve collaboration and active engagement with content.

In this chapter, we report the findings from our qualitative research about teaching and learning in TILE classrooms that was conducted in the spring and fall semesters of 2011. Recognizing that prior research had demonstrated that learning environments like TILE classrooms were powerful instructional tools (for example, Beichner et al. 2007; Brooks 2011), we decided that qualitative research methods were best suited for our purpose of investigating in detail the processes of designing and implementing instruction in TILE classrooms. Marshall and Rossman (2010) point out that one of the characteristics of a qualitative study is that it focuses on the contexts of activity.

The main purpose of our research project was twofold. First, we wanted to learn about how and why instructors in TILE classrooms implemented

Table 2.1. Number of Procedures for Each Semester of Research Study

	Spring 2011	Fall 2011
Pre-semester interviews with instructors	6	7
Post-semester interviews with instructors	6	7
Student focus groups	7	6
Classroom observations	128	155

specific learning activities in the TILE classroom and how students perceived the usefulness of these activities. Second, we intended to synthesize our findings for our colleagues in ITS-Instructional Services to help them improve faculty development and the overall administration of TILE classrooms.

Research Methods

Our qualitative research methods enabled the researchers (Van Horne, Murniati, and Saichaie 2012) to collect rich descriptions of how instructors adapted their teaching strategies to fit the unique attributes of the TILE classrooms, how students participated in learning activities, and what students believed was beneficial about taking classes in TILE classrooms. We conducted semistructured interviews with each instructor at the beginning and end of the semester to learn about their attitudes toward teaching in a TILE classroom. We facilitated student focus groups to learn about what students believed was helpful and not as helpful about their activities in a TILE classroom. Lastly, we developed an observation protocol for documenting instructional activities. See Table 2.1 for a breakdown of the number of procedures carried out for each semester of the research study. (See the appendix of Van Horne, Murniati, and Saichaie [2012] for observation and interview protocols.)

For each case, the transcriptions, observations, and field notes were the basis of our preliminary coding across cases. From the interviews, focus groups, and class observations, we were able to extract emerging themes, such as reasons for using the TILE classrooms, the advantages of the room, technology-related problems, collaborative learning activities, and many other themes that pertain to teaching and learning in the TILE classrooms. The use of interviews, focus groups, and class observations has enabled us to answer our research questions from differing points of views; thus, we were able to maintain the trustworthiness of our study (Creswell 2003).

The Need for a Better Environment for Student-Centered Learning Activities

The TILE classrooms enabled instructors to use teaching methods that they believed could not be supported in regular "general assignment" (that is, traditional) classrooms at the University of Iowa. In this section, we describe the experiences of two instructors, Professors Ackerman and Gallagher, who were part of a larger mixed-methods research study about the effectiveness of the TILE classrooms and the "fit" of learning activity and learning environment (see Van Horne, Murniati, and Saichaie 2012).

Both professors' teaching practices highlight some of the larger themes that emerged from our complete data sets: (1) instructors redesigned activities in collaborative learning environments by incorporating the learning tools and the technology in the TILE classrooms, (2) activities in the TILE classrooms work well when there is a mechanism to make sure that students prepared the materials prior to coming to class and stay on tasks during the class activities, and (3) students benefit greatly from the TILE environment when instructors give students more authority for sharing their work.

Professor Ackerman wanted to teach her undergraduate research methods course in a TILE classroom because when she had taught the course previously, the final grades had a bimodal distribution. She said in the first interview, "I wanted to try something new to see if I could get those kids who are not engaged in the course . . . to be a little more involved because it is a required course for them" (personal interview, February 22, 2011). She revamped the course so that the contents of her materials and the activities fit the design of the classroom. Professor Ackerman planned to supplement each lecture with collaborative activity so that students could apply what they had learned about the different research methods. For example, on one day early in the semester, Professor Ackerman facilitated an activity about the concepts of deduction and induction. The students used the laptops (working in small groups of three) to access web pages about Oscar nominations. Students analyzed the arguments in small groups, wrote up their results, and submitted them through the course management system. She then displayed the different answers on the screens and led a whole-group discussion in which most students participated. Professor Ackerman said that such activities appeared to motivate students who were reluctant to engage in the early part of the semester: "I just think it is about group interaction and giving kids something challenging and fun and kind of following up on it. And they bought into the system" (personal interview, May 23, 2011).

Professor Gallagher, who was teaching two courses in the TILE classroom during the semester she was in the study, decided to teach an undergraduate course about race in the TILE classroom because she had already planned a graduate course for the TILE classroom (personal interview, January 19, 2011). Originally, she had planned to teach just the graduate course in a TILE classroom because she wanted to "[get] the graduate students involved in active learning techniques, so that they could use them in their own classes." She emphasized that the TILE classroom would enable her to "model" these teaching strategies for her students. But she also decided to teach an undergraduate class in a TILE classroom so that her students could engage in research activities that were not possible in a traditional classroom environment. In her first interview, she stated that she appreciated how easy it would be to move around the classroom and work one-to-one with students during discussion or group activities.

In addition, Professor Gallagher expected to be able to do various activities that she could not do in her previous courses. For example, she often had students examine Census data that were related to a specific theme, but this had been an out-of-class activity for students. Using a web-based program for data analysis, students collaborated in groups of three while they developed hypotheses and tested them. In her graduate course, students often engaged in class discussion about issues related to the design of instruction.

Our different qualitative research methods were useful in determining the value of the new design of instruction that Professor Gallagher employed in the TILE classroom. We observed a variety of ways that groups engaged in collaborative behavior. For example, in one class period, the students were analyzing Census data related to segregation in American cities. They used the wall-mounted monitors to display tables that included their analyses of the data. Using a cooperative learning strategy from the faculty-development program, the students worked in groups of three in which each person was a manager, a skeptic, or a recorder. (The manager helped keep the group on task; the skeptic questioned the group's findings and proposed alternative explanations; and the recorder kept notes about the activity.) In groups, the students practiced making hypotheses and discussing the results of their cross-tabulations. The professor and teaching assistant walked around the room, consulting with each group about certain results.

In Professor Ackerman's course, students worked actively together in groups at the round tables, though the wall-mounted monitors were not essential. In a typical class, the professor would lecture about a concept in the course, and students would then work together in groups on the laptop. They would download an assignment to work on together, use the laptop or whiteboard, and then upload their completed activity to the learning management system. Thus, the TILE classroom afforded the instructor a flexible learning environment to seamlessly move from a lecture to a student-centered activity in which students could take advantage of a variety of different tools.

Throughout the research project, the qualitative research methods were important for learning about how students interacted while using the group roles (recorder, manager, and skeptic). For example, we observed situations in which students were not engaged in these special group activities. In one observation, the student playing the role of the "recorder" was not engaged in the analysis of the data. Rather, this person functionally played the exclusive role of a scribe. Professor Gallagher had decided to rotate regularly the assignment of group roles the next time she taught this course. We reported de-identified summaries of our observations to our colleagues so that they can refine the faculty-development program to enable instructors to use collaborative learning more effectively. The faculty-development team, in turn, began to emphasize the potential pitfalls of cooperative learning in the TILE classroom and used examples from the assessment to assist faculty members in attending to the composition of groups in collaborative learning activities. In addition, members of the assessment team gave presentations to faculty during training sessions to provide examples of effective collaborative learning strategies in TILE classrooms and how to plan for cases in which students are disengaged.

In their final interviews, both participants emphasized how teaching in the TILE learning environment had improved their instruction. Professor Gallagher said that the TILE environment had revolutionized her way of teaching her undergraduate course. With students doing the data analysis in class, she was able to provide feedback earlier, observe where students had difficulty with data analysis, and better prepare students for future assignments. In her final interview she said, "But because it was in the room, I could intervene and fix that as we were going along, and I didn't have to, you know, get a bunch of confused writing assignments" (personal interview, April 28, 2011). And Professor Ackerman indicated that students came to her office hours less that semester, which supported her own impression that the student-centered activities were better at helping students understand the concepts in research methods (personal interview, May 23, 2011). In addition, she reported that students who did not actively participate in the beginning of the course became more confident in contributing their ideas during group discussions and class discussions throughout the course. She noticed that improved student engagement was possibly due to the compulsory group work. She indicated that group work encouraged students to contribute more because every student realized he or she had a stake. Their voices were heard. They were not ignored. Students who did not attend in-class collaborative activities eventually realized that other group members suffered from their absence.

Faculty Development for TILE Instructors

Both of these faculty members had undergone training in the TILE Faculty Institute. This three-day, intensive workshop was modeled on a format developed by the Center for Teaching in 2005 and implemented seven times since. Faculty Institute participants learn specific pedagogical theories and strategies; they are then responsible for creating new courses that incorporate those pedagogies and teaching the courses at least three times during a three-year period. The Institute format has provided a springboard for the rapid but thoughtful adoption of new pedagogies as well as the creation of a significant number of new high-impact practice courses at Iowa.

As the TILE project began, it became apparent that creative classroom design and sophisticated technology alone would not ensure the optimal learning experience for students. In fact, because students sit at round tables and the rooms lack a front focal point, the traditional lecture format can be counterproductive in these active learning spaces. To help faculty members maximize student learning, we decided to focus the Institute training on three pedagogical strategies: in-class, team-based learning; peer instruction; and inquiry-guided learning. Both of these participants emphasized that faculty development was essential to their success; Professor Ackerman said that the training was "essential" and would not recommend that anyone try teaching in a TILE classroom without that kind of support (personal interview, May 23, 2011).

The Challenges Instructors Face in TILE Classrooms

In addition to the successes of these instructors, our observations and interviews uncovered the difficulties that instructors faced in the TILE classrooms. For example, Professor Gallagher expressed that her new teaching strategies were much more time intensive. During one observation, the lead author observed the students working in groups to summarize different sections of a reading that was completed by the entire class. Although the students were engaged in the discussion of the themes of the reading, Professor Gallagher went around the room trying to remind students of the deadline. She remarked in the final interview that student-centered activities often took more time than she had allotted. In her final interview, she stated that she had "underestimated" the difficulty of the collaborative tasks (personal interview, April 28, 2011). Professor Ackerman's reflections on the collaborative tasks corroborated Professor Gallagher's statement. She indicated that in order to be actively engaged in collaborative tasks, students had to prepare the materials outside of class. Students who prepared in advance would come to class feeling more confident and would be able to contribute more significantly to the discussions.

We also learned about the teaching strategies that instructors did not think were a good fit for the TILE classroom. Professor Gallagher commented that the TILE classroom was not a good environment for a class discussion because people could not see each other. Based on the observations, this was more of an issue in the graduate course that was more centered on discussion than the undergraduate course. Professor Gallagher, indeed, decided that other graduate courses could be taught in a department seminar room because these students would not be engaging in collaborative problem solving.

Both professors emphasized that preparing a course for the TILE classroom is very time consuming. Professor Ackerman, though she had a positive experience in the TILE classroom, said that she was not ready, at that time, to redesign another one of her courses so that it would be a good fit for the TILE classroom. Citing the fact that she worked at an "R1" institution, she indicated that she needed to devote more time to her scholarship. Thus, she planned to continue to teach her research methods course in a TILE classroom, but she said she would not be redesigning another course for some time (personal interview, May 23, 2011). Professor Gallagher also said it was a "time-consuming" activity to redesign a course to change the activities from lecture-based teaching strategies to those that involve more student construction of knowledge. She said, "I want them to [learn] about institutional racism without me just saying 'Here's what institutional racism looks like'" (personal interview, April 28, 2011). Although she wanted to continue to make her course more activity based, she stressed that she only had time to change a little at a time. Both instructors indicated that they would like to see more faculty members adopt the TILE classrooms, but also recognized that the time commitment would be an impediment.

Conclusion and Implications

The results of our research project indicate that qualitative research is a valuable tool for understanding how students and instructors participate in learning activities in the TILE classroom. For the instructors highlighted here, the TILE classrooms provided a classroom setting that enabled the facilitation of collaborative learning and the use of pedagogies that were not possible in traditional classroom environments. We developed detailed descriptions of effective instructional design, and this information has been useful in developing new training materials for faculty that are beginning to teach in TILE classrooms.

A broader lesson from the TILE experience at the University of Iowa concerns the importance of research-based faculty development in the use of such spaces. From an institutional perspective, we have learned that faculty development is essential to the success of TILE. Faculty who know how to use the technology and the features of the rooms, and to plan their courses accordingly, produce better student outcomes. Clearly, each instructor in this study gained experience in the use of active learning pedagogies and developed knowledge about what techniques are most effective. Qualitative research such as this is critical to bringing that information to a wider audience.

One implication of this research is that Instructional Services can help instructors to develop learning activities that are particularly suited to the kind of learning that professors want to happen in their TILE courses. Professors reported in our interviews that converting units from lecture-based activities to collaborative-learning activities is time consuming. Indeed, Professor Gallagher said that she only converted a portion of her class to include activities that were appropriate for the TILE classroom. And yet, students were engaged and interested when they were participating in authentic activities—which suggests that the university should provide additional support for instructors who want to redesign their teaching to promote student engagement.

The TILE Initiative originated during a period when the University of Iowa could have turned away from creating dynamic learning environments and focused solely on creating more classrooms that are not as suited for technology-supported collaborative learning. We believe that the TILE Initiative will continue to grow and prosper in part because it was forged in a difficult time when it would have been easy to turn away from change. Now, academic units (such as the College of Pharmacy) across campus are embracing the TILE model and we are confident that these learning environments and the faculty-development program have become an essential element of the fabric of learning at the University of Iowa.

References

Beichner, R., J. Saul, D. Abbott, J. Morse, D. Deardorff, R. Allain, S. Bonham, M. Dancy, and J. Risley. 2007. "Student-Centered Activities for Large Enrollment Undergraduate Programs (SCALE-UP) Project." In *Research-Based Reform of University Physics*, edited by E. F. Redish and P. J. Cooney, 1–42. College Park, MD: American Association of Physics Teachers.

Brooks, D. C. 2011. "Space Matters: The Impact of Formal Learning Environments on Student Learning." *British Journal of Educational Technology* 42 (5): 719–726.

Creswell, J. W. 2003. *Research Design: Qualitative, Quantitative, and Mixed Method Approaches*. Thousand Oaks, CA: Sage Publications.

Marshall, C., and G. B. Rossman. 2010. *Designing Qualitative Research*. London: Sage Publications.

Van Horne, S., C. Murniati, and K. Saichaie. 2012. "Assessing Teaching and Learning in Technology-Infused TILE Classrooms at the University of Iowa." *Seeking Evidence of Impact*. Accessed May 1, 2013. http://www.educause.edu/library/resources/assessing-teaching-and-learning-technology-infused-tile-classrooms-university-iowa.

SAM VAN HORNE *is an assessment coordinator in ITS-Instructional Services and the Office of the Provost at the University of Iowa.*

CECILIA TITIEK MURNIATI *is a faculty member and the vice dean for Academic Affairs in the Faculty of Languages and Arts at Soegijapranata Catholic University, Semarang, Indonesia. She also currently serves as an ad hoc member for the Board of National Education Standardization in Indonesia.*

KEM SAICHAIE *is the director of Educational Environment and Technology for the Center for Teaching and Faculty Development at the University of Massachusetts–Amherst.*

MAGGIE JESSE is the senior director of the University of Iowa's ITS-Instructional Services, chairs the campus-wide Academic Technology Advisory Council, and serves as a facilitator for the Learning Spaces Executive Committee.

JEAN C. FLORMAN is the director of the University of Iowa Center for Teaching.

BETH F. INGRAM is the Tippie Professor of Economics, dean of University College, and associate provost for Undergraduate Education at The University of Iowa.

NEW DIRECTIONS FOR TEACHING AND LEARNING • DOI: 10.1002/tl

3

This chapter explores the "educational alliance" among students and between students and instructors. We contend that this is a framework that can help us understand how active learning classrooms facilitate positive educational outcomes.

Active Learning Classrooms and Educational Alliances: Changing Relationships to Improve Learning

Paul Baepler, J. D. Walker

Introduction

A growing body of research on the impact of newly configured, technology-enhanced learning spaces shows that these classrooms can have a variety of positive effects on teaching and learning at the postsecondary level, including improvements in student affect and motivation, student engagement, and student learning outcomes (Beichner et al. 2007; Brooks 2011, 2012; Dori and Belcher 2005; Walker, Brooks, and Baepler 2011; Whiteside, Brooks, and Walker, 2010). One question that arises on the heels of these results has to do with *mechanisms*. How, or in virtue of what, do new learning spaces have the effects they do? Under what conditions will the impact of new learning spaces be enhanced or mitigated?

This chapter describes research into one potential mechanism through which new learning spaces may influence teaching and learning, namely, changes in interpersonal classroom relationships. Amedeo, Golledge, and Stimson (2009) theorized that space "exerts significant influences on [human activity and experiencing] through complex and intricate relationships" (12). We hypothesize that newly designed classrooms can alter in-class dynamics in two basic ways: first, by breaking down the hierarchies that divide teachers and learners in traditional learning spaces, and second, by fostering greater affinity among students. To put the point differently, new learning spaces can facilitate *educational alliances* between students and instructors and among students, *relationships* that help to improve both the student learning experience and the learning outcomes that students achieve.

NEW DIRECTIONS FOR TEACHING AND LEARNING, no. 137, Spring 2014 © 2014 Wiley Periodicals, Inc.
Published online in Wiley Online Library (wileyonlinelibrary.com) • DOI: 10.1002/tl.20083

The research described here is preliminary in the sense that it draws on both existing and new data on learning spaces. We argue that these data are consistent with, and generally supportive of, the existence of an association between newly designed classrooms and classroom alliances, and we map future directions for this line of research that center on the development and application of direct, validated measures of educational alliance.

Data and Methods

To conduct this study, we needed a conceptual framework that would systematize our investigation of classroom relationships, focusing on the aspects of those relationships that are educationally crucial. We located such a framework in the notion of the *educational alliance.*

The concept of interpersonal alliances was originally brought forward in the field of psychotherapy (Bordin 1979) and later adapted to the context of the college classroom (Billson and Tiberius 1991; Meyers 2008; Tiberius and Billson 1991). The focus on alliance is built on the general proposition that the social context in which teaching and learning takes place can affect, either positively or negatively, student academic and developmental outcomes. Several decades of educational theory and empirical evidence support this proposition, suggesting that such factors as student involvement in academic life, substantive student contact with faculty and with peers, faculty enthusiasm and expressiveness, reciprocity among students, and a cooperative classroom context can improve student motivation, achievement, and persistence (Chickering and Gamson 1991; Endo and Harpel 1982; Pascarella and Terenzini 2005; Tiberius 1993–1994; Tiberius and Billson 1991; Tinto 1997).

In this study, we adopted Tiberius and Billson's (1991) conception of the educational alliance in relatively intact form. In their examination of the social context of teaching and learning, Tiberius and Billson considered several prominent empirical-theoretical perspectives on education in an effort to identify the specific aspects of the educational context that are crucial to establishing mutually reinforcing social bonds in the classroom. They concluded that the key features of educational alliance are as follows:

1. mutual respect,
2. shared responsibility for·learning,
3. effective communication and feedback,
4. cooperation, and
5. trust and security.

While Tiberius and Billson (1991) focused primarily on the social arrangements *between students and teachers,* however, we believe that the concept of alliance can be usefully extended to include relationships *among students,* particularly in learning spaces like the active learning classrooms

(ALCs), in which evidence from past studies strongly suggests that the student-student social dynamic is powerful (Walker, Brooks, and Baepler 2011).

The data used in this study were gathered from students and faculty at the University of Minnesota between 2008 and 2012 using the following methods:

- Large-scale student and faculty surveys conducted in fall 2008, spring 2011, and spring 2012 ($n = 2,060$).
- Eight semistructured interviews with faculty who taught in ALCs in spring 2012.
- A faculty focus group conducted in spring 2012.
- A student focus group conducted in spring 2012.

Survey data derive from both closed and open-ended questions; the survey instruments were validated and tested for reliability.[1] Our process for utilizing the data began with examining our data-collection tools to locate questions the answers to which might bear, negatively or positively, on the hypothesis that a class's being taught in an ALC promotes one or more of the five features of educational alliance. Two researchers then examined the data identified in this way and collaboratively aligned the data points with the most closely associated features of educational alliance.

Findings

Using the process described above, we found many indications from multiple data sources that the ALCs do indeed conduce to the development of alliances between students and instructors, and among students themselves. And we found very few indications to the contrary. Overall, this investigation contributes to the theory of educational alliances, suggesting that new learning spaces designed to enhance group interaction might signal a new social context and alter classroom conduct.

Dimension 1: Mutual Respect.   In their landmark report *How People Learn*, Bransford, Brown, and Cocking (2000) described the importance of creating a learning environment that is "community centered" (144) and in which the classroom forms a community. Chickering and Gamson (1991) also encouraged both formal and informal contact between instructor and students as a good practice in higher education, suggesting that such interaction "enhances students' intellectual commitment" (65). The educational alliance codifies these principles under the dimension of establishing mutual respect, and we provide evidence to show that the ALCs foster mutual respect by creating a classroom environment that is *informal*, *relaxed*, and *egalitarian*.

Informality, Intimacy, and Immediacy.   By design, the ALCs do not project an obvious front-to-back hierarchy. Typically, the instructor's podium is somewhere in the middle, and students may naturally pass near it when they enter or leave the class. Combined with easier access to any seat in the room, this feature creates opportunities for impromptu conversations. One instructor commented, "There was definitely more of an intimacy with the tables, a little bit more pre-class chatter, where [before] I was kind of behind this big, huge podium in the traditional class." Another instructor who criticized one ALC for locating the rostrum next to a wall put it, "I think for me a lot of the benefit of the classroom has to do with people seeing people, and I think this [locating the podium next to a wall] doesn't get at that really at all."

Sometimes making a large classroom seem smaller simply by interacting with students more closely and more frequently can change the dynamic. One instructor reasoned,

> I think it's maybe a peculiar function of the way human beings work but if we were, you know, this close, and nothing bad happened, and this happens often enough, I'd just feel more comfortable coming to your office and talking to you or I'd be more comfortable saying something that has nothing to do with class or it's—you're kind of friends at this point. You've seen a lot of each other; they know my mannerisms, I know some of theirs.

In their 2005 research review, *How College Affects Students*, Pascarella and Terenzini reported that informal contact among students and between instructors and students plays a critical role in socialization on campus. The effect of these interactions "was manifest in intellectual outcomes as well as in changes in attitudes, values, aspirations, and a number of psychosocial characteristics" (613).

Student survey data from several different classes support the idea that the ALCs strengthen bonds and support among students. Students in the ALC sections of three classes agreed significantly more strongly than students in non-ALC sections of the same classes that their classroom helped them to develop connections with their instructor (see Table 3.1).

Relaxed Atmosphere. One instructor remarked that it takes an extremely skilled lecturer to interact casually with students and even joke around with them from the podium of a lecture hall. For her, the ALC was

> much more like sitting around your living room talking with somebody and it just feels more informal; we're getting a lot of work done. It's not that we're goofing off in class; we're covering a lot of serious topics and students are uncovering a lot of content, but the fact that I can just walk among them … changes the way faculty and students look at each other I think.

By placing students in a position in which everyone can see, and be seen by, everyone else in the room, the ALCs seem to create a kind of psychological and emotional immediacy often lacking in traditional classrooms. This dynamic can foster respect among students of the sort

Table 3.1. Student Survey Responses to Connections with Instructor

The classroom in which I am taking this course helps me to...

Question	Course	Classroom	Mean	Standard Deviation	N	t Statistic
... develop	PSTL 1135	Traditional	2.97	.627	34	−.857
connections with		ALC	3.11	.758	35	
my instructor	BIOL 1003	Traditional	2.61	.715	163	−2.902**
		ALC	2.88	.791	101	
	CHEM 1061	Traditional	2.36	.734	209	−6.344***
		ALC	2.80	.706	220	

Note: Questions were answered using a four-point Likert scale in which *strongly agree* = 4 and *strongly disagree* = 1.
$**p < .01, ***p < .001.$

observed by one instructor in a class that dealt with difficult, emotionally charged issues of gender and sex:

> I think [the students] are very respectful to each other ... and even when things [become tense] ... the women were, like, they were really directing it right at him and he had to deal with their anger and their affect coming at his direction and ... you can see each other, right, in a different way and I think that mattered and that matters."

Egalitarianism.   The disruption of the traditional spatial hierarchy fosters new opportunities for conversations. One professor noted, "I like the fact that I can be anywhere in the classroom, nobody feels that they're in a segregated spot compared to another spot. I think that's valuable." Another instructor reframed the challenge her class faced in hearing one another as an opportunity to coach mutual respect, "I can acknowledge ... how incredibly difficult it is to listen to one person in that large group, but how important it is, and how we have to kind of all make this sort of pact, you know, that we're going to respect our peers and me when we're talking."

Two survey questions delivered in 2012 provided information relevant to the matter of mutual respect. One question asked students whether their classroom helped them to "understand someone else's views by imagining how an issue looks from his or her perspective"; the other asked whether their classroom assisted them in "growing comfortable working with people from other cultures." Students in a large, ALC-taught section of introductory chemistry agreed significantly more strongly with both propositions than students in a near-identical section of the same class taught in a traditional room (see Table 3.2).

Dimension 2: Shared Responsibility for Learning.   The idea that learners bear some responsibility for their own learning is a crucial part of moving away from the metaphor of learning in which the learner is a

Table 3.2. 2012 Student Survey Responses to Questions Aligned with Mutual Respect

The classroom in which I am taking this course helps me to . . .

Question	Course	Classroom	Mean	Standard Deviation	N	t Statistic
. . . understand someone else's views . . .	CHEM 1061	Traditional	2.34	.668	208	−7.130***
		ALC	2.80	.681	218	
. . . grow comfortable working with people from other cultures	CHEM 1061	Traditional	2.36	.701	209	−8.324***
		ALC	2.91	.664	219	

Note: Questions were answered using a four-point Likert scale in which *strongly agree* = 4 and *strongly disagree* = 1.
***$p < .001$.

vessel into which knowledge is poured. As Billson and Tiberius (1991) wrote, "Making the shift from being a passive learner to an active one depends in large part on one's increasing willingness to accept shared responsibility for one's own educational experience" (92). The ALCs facilitate this process both by encouraging active, group-centered teaching-learning methods and by placing students in a situation in which they are accountable to their peers at least as much as to the instructor. The evidence in this section is organized around the notions of *interdependence* and the *reduction of passivity.*

Mutual Interdependence and Accountability. Several instructors described instances when students called upon each other to change their behavior, effectively asserting control over the flow of events in the classroom. For instance, it is not uncommon for students in the larger ALCs to ask students to repeat comments into the microphone so that everyone could hear what someone was saying, despite the fact that many students are reluctant to broadcast their voice. One instructor noted, "In the ALC, they definitely were more in control of what was happening in the classroom . . . I mean, I wasn't even part of it."

Some instructors encourage this type of response by listing what good group members do, such as learn each other's names, exchange contact information, and arrive to class on time. The focus of responsibility shifts somewhat from the teacher-student relationship to one among peers. The group matters more than the individual. As one instructor put it, "I would say, you know, to the extent they're forced to do things; they're not forced to do them in response to me so much as to their peers."

In fact, leadership in groups in the ALCs can be so diffused that it is difficult to detect from the outside. One instructor commented, "[more] leaders emerged in the traditional room than maybe I saw in the ALC. Like

I had whole tables where I could not have told you who the definitive leader was, because they were all talking."

Diluting Passivity.   The nonhierarchical layout of the ALCs appears to block a dynamic that is common in lecture halls, in which students who are inclined to be passive and want to avoid responsibility for their own learning gather in certain parts of the classroom—usually in the back. In the view of one instructor, the ALCs disrupt this arrangement in a useful way:

> I feel different because it's a friendlier environment because I'm not thinking that the nerds are in the front and the people in the back don't care. There are people who don't care but they're sprinkled in with other people and they're everywhere.

One instructor described the difference in striking terms, saying that in the ALCs,

> I wouldn't be looking at a *passive-aggressive gradient* [emphasis added] .... there is a gradient in the room and you feel like you're working against that ... perception that they want to be anonymous in the back ... And what's really different is that there is no back row so students are around the tables and I have no preconceived notion ... of what their level of engagement is based on where they're sitting."

Dimension 3: Effective Communication and Feedback.   Chickering and Gamson (1991) underlined the importance of developing strong communication between students and instructors as well as giving students prompt feedback on their performance. The educational alliance framework adopts these principles as a single key feature, and many aspects of the ALC design promote effective communication and feedback, in particular *proximity*, *new lines of communication,* the use of appropriate *technology*, and the promotion of *higher quality communication.*

Physical Proximity.   For instance, because circular tables are substituted for rows of fixed seats and aisles, instructors are able to move through the room and stand next to any student. One instructor commented, "If you feel like you need to connect with your students then you have to be moving around," and the open design of the ALCs allows an instructor to weave through the classroom to consult with groups of students and comment on their work.

New Avenues for Communication.   The ALCs appear to foster multiple channels of communication, including productive conversations among students rather than just between instructor and students. One instructor said,

> Typically, in the traditional room, everything's got to be fed through me .... [In the ALCs] They were having dialogs with their peers ... there'd be times

when I was nowhere in the line of sight of groups of students who were communicating with each other [using the table microphones], which was awesome.

This manner of conducting class puts a primacy on communication and feedback, and the same seating pattern that makes group work easy—using numbered round tables—also makes it simple to manage. As one teacher explained,

So I have three different ways I can call on someone; either by the whole table, by a pod of three within a table, or I can spy a name card and say, hey "Joe," what did your pod decide?

As another instructor put it,

I have always tried to figure out a way that I could somehow get more feedback from the class, what have you really gotten out of this; what have you been following, not following. And so I think the active learning classroom has facilitated the ability to get more student feedback to me about what they think, what's their response to a problem. Would it be as easy to do that in a traditional classroom? It wouldn't be as easy.

Technology and Physical Features.   The ALCs' technology also seems to aid communication. Because each table has its own whiteboard widescreen monitor next to it, some instructors asked students to display their work. One teacher required every table to draw a concept map of a particularly vexing process, saying, "I want to see what you've been thinking about." The same instructor would use manipulables, asking students to create models of cell structures. She mentioned that the ability to do this in class was due to the simple function of "having space on the table to lay things out." This tabletop space allowed students to demonstrate their knowledge in a manner that could be easily scanned by the instructor, giving her a sense for how students conceived of the material and allowing her to adjust her remarks accordingly.

Higher Quality of Communication.   Several instructors mentioned that when teaching in the ALCs, they often felt like they lost control of some aspects of the class, because students asked quite different questions from the ones they expected to receive, possibly because the questions had been preprocessed in small group discussions. This change meant that there was "less scriptedness" and that "you have to respond and be ready in a different way, kind of be on the balls of your feet." "Get ready not to know everything," is the way one teacher put it.

They would ask more sophisticated questions. And it could be because in a group of three to nine people, they really quickly established what they knew already. They wouldn't waste the whole class's time. They'd figure it out on their own, in their groups, and then the questions they asked me were like … I was totally unprepared for them.

This change in the quality of communication will again become relevant in the Trust and Security dimension mentioned below.

Dimension 4: Cooperation.   Overwhelming empirical evidence, particularly since the 1970s, has demonstrated that among college-age students, cooperative learning promotes higher individual achievement than competitive or individualistic learning (Johnson, Johnson, and Smith 2007). While instructors have long called upon students to cooperate on projects and assignments, the physical configuration of the ALCs, in particular the round tables, is designed to facilitate just this sort of pedagogy. The evidence in this section bears on the ALCs' tendency to foster *cooperative educational practices* and *bonding and support* among students.

Cooperative Teaching-Learning Practices.   A chemistry instructor commented, "It's good to have the right configuration of the room, but it's also really good to sort of force people to take on roles that meet the intent of the [ALC]." This understanding of the space convinced the professor to assign seating in the classroom even before the first day of class began. This allowed him to define nine roles for examining professional articles:

> If your seat letter is this, you're expected to be doing this and then it rotates as we go through papers, and, you know, that has worked particularly well because nobody at the table gets to just sit there and listen passively.

The process worked so well, in fact, that one day in midsemester, when the professor was unforeseeably late to class by five minutes, the groups had already started reviewing the week's articles when he arrived. The same instructor, however, lamented the behavior he saw in an experimental group midterm. Students divided the content ahead of the exam and specialized in singular areas, which resulted in individual students knowing narrow spectrums of the material deeply and, perhaps, lacking a broader understanding.

Other instructors would take advantage of the table groupings to engage in constructive controversies. Teams of students would engage a task and compete against another. For instance, in a gender and sexuality studies course, debates were assigned:

> We used the class time to plan what they were going to say and they could project their documents on their individual table projector systems and each work on their own component. They could also walk over to the other tables and share; so an argument could share with a counter argument because they could be at tables next to each other. So the physical space of the room is perfect for doing things like debates where they're all working on different components but that are interrelated so that they want to share materials.

Table 3.3. Student Survey Responses to a Question Regarding Bonds between Students

The classroom in which I am taking this course helps me to ...

Question	Course	Classroom	Mean	Standard Deviation	N	t Statistic
... develop connections with my classmates	PSTL 1135	Traditional	3.15	.657	34	−2.137*
		ALC	3.49	.658	35	
	BIOL 1003	Traditional	2.91	.734	162	−5.242***
		ALC	3.38	.630	101	
	CHEM 1061	Traditional	2.32	.690	210	−12.073***
		ALC	3.10	.657	220	

Note: Questions were answered using a four-point Likert scale in which *strongly agree* = 4 and *strongly disagree* = 1.
*p<.05, ***p < .001.

Student Bonding and Support.   These comments by faculty were echoed by students. In one of our focus groups, there was universal agreement that the ALCs fostered greater bonding among students, a sense that students were all in it together. One student summed it up: "I think the group setting helped us create good friendships. I still talk to a couple of the people from that class." The sense of mutual support created by the round tables was a focus of comments by students in our student surveys: "It was great having a group of nine kids to whom I could always utilize in my time of need to bounce ideas off of." Instructors also observed the development of connections among students: "[The ALC] changes the kind of nuanced ways people connect to each other. So they respond to each other differently and . . . I think there is that different sense of community that affects experience with relation to each other."

Finally, student survey data from several classes support the idea that the ALCs strengthen bonds and support among students. Students in the ALC sections of three different classes agreed significantly more strongly than students in non-ALC sections of the same classes that their classroom helped them to develop connections with their classmates (see Table 3.3). Similar results emerged by an analysis of survey responses from students in a large chemistry course taught in 2012 in an ALC, with respect to the issue whether their classroom helped them to develop confidence working in small groups (see Table 3.4).

Dimension 5: Trust and Security.   Creating a safe learning environment in which students feel able to express their views freely is crucial to maintaining active student engagement in the learning process. An unsafe classroom atmosphere will cause self-censoring and the preemptive stifling of student participation, reducing both the amount of processing students engage in and the quality and quantity of feedback they receive. We found that the ALCs foster, in the words of one instructor, "a safe climate [in

Table 3.4. Student Survey Responses to a Question about Working in Small Groups of Students

The classroom in which I am taking this course helps me to . . .

Question	Course	Classroom	Mean	Standard Deviation	N	t Statistic
. . . develop confidence working in small groups.	CHEM 1061	Traditional	2.17	.768	210	−14.925***
		ALC	3.18	.626	221	

Note: Question was answered using a four-point Likert scale in which *strongly agree* = 4 and *strongly disagree* = 1.
***$p < .001$.

which] students . . . feel more comfortable about displaying either ignorance or knowledge." However, the evidence in support of this feature of educational alliance is weaker than the evidence for the other four features. It comes in the form of changed classroom dynamics including a *gradual immersion* in class material, making space for *being wrong*, and a tendency toward *disruption and surveillance* in the classroom.

Gradual Immersion. Because the round tables and movable chairs make small conversations feel natural, the ALCs can also help scaffold more initially uncomfortable material. In a zoology class that focuses on sex, for instance, the instructor intentionally worked up to topics like infanticide or disproportionate murder ratios in men over women.

> We had some really good conversations about some really, really tricky material in the ALC. And I like to think that—or it's easy for me to think that it's because they were comfortable with the talking they'd already done in their small groups.

Another instructor in a gender studies course mentioned that when talking about rape, she did not want to have her back to anyone in the room. She purposefully situated herself in the corner of a room with a microphone so she could watch facial expressions, and then she gradually moved toward the center of the room.

> It actually, I think, still allowed this feeling of intimacy even though I had removed myself from the center . . . I circle the table in the middle and I walk towards certain tables and off to other tables, [and it] allows them to kind of feel like I'm there with them in a way that I think is closer and much more like a smaller room experience, almost like a discussion section at times.

Being Wrong. The ALCs introduce a classroom dynamic in which students often ask questions that are more sophisticated and more probing than the typical question in a traditional room. While this situation can be uncomfortable for teachers new to the ALCs, it also provides an opportunity to model the process of professional academic inquiry for students in which being wrong is not only acceptable but also an expected part of the knowledge-creation enterprise. As one instructor said,

> We're all doing this together and … they do ask questions that I don't know the answer to and … it feels much more comfortable to say, that is a really good, probing question and there's probably someone who has done some research on that. [It's not that] you just embarrassed me by asking me something I didn't know the answer to. We're exploring this together and I think it's kind of cool that you asked something that I don't know the answer to.

Disruption and Surveillance.   At times, the lack of a physical center of focus in the room and the disorder that stems from exploratory activities can create a bit of chaos, and an instructor needs to learn how to work with that. That disruptions may occur more frequently as instructors modulate between group activities and microlectures suggests that the room may not inherently foster a sense of security without guidance.

The challenge, then, becomes reestablishing order and using the properties of the space to maintain a strong learning environment. For instance, the fact that students do not all face in a single direction with their backs to each other changes the dynamic. "Nobody ever falls asleep in this class because they're in the panopticon," one instructor commented, referencing Jeremy Bentham's term for a building that encourages self-surveillance.

> In a panopticon, everybody can see them. I can see them. So there is that sense that the surveillance level is different than in a lecture hall where there is a more passive role that they assume … there's much more of a sense that their peers are all paying attention, we're all paying attention, she can see me, we're engaged.

Safety and trust, in this regard, are borne out of establishing what Billson and Tiberius (1991) termed new "group norms" and become "self-reinforcing," particularly when recognized by students and encouraged by the instructor.

Conclusion

On the basis of existing evidence, we conclude that ALCs tend to change the social context of classes taught in these rooms in constructive ways. In particular, ALCs are well suited for fostering educational alliances between instructors and students, and among students themselves. Although the comparative evidence is scant, we also conclude that ALCs are likely to provide better support for educational alliances than traditional classrooms. The ALCs, however, are not a magical solution; they must be used well in order to bring about their good effects (see, for example, Chapter 5), and

NEW DIRECTIONS FOR TEACHING AND LEARNING • DOI: 10.1002/tl

their structure has the potential for its own disruptions of classroom relationships, such as disruption and the sense of surveillance described in the previous section.

It should be emphasized again that our conclusions are only provisional, because they are based on a secondary analysis of both existing and new data, rather than on data collected for the express purpose of assessing social contexts in different types of classrooms. The next step, therefore, is to develop a valid and reliable measure for measuring educational alliances in the classroom and to apply it within a research design that will allow us to draw comparative conclusions (Tichenor and Hill 1989). We have begun this process with a field trial of a draft instrument designed to measure educational alliances. We also plan further data gathering through faculty interviews and student focus groups that will center directly on the notion of classroom social context.

The instigation of this line of inquiry stemmed from instructors' observations about the changed nature of social relations in the active learning classrooms. Should our provisional findings hold true upon further measurement and analysis, we foresee the ability to design faculty development recommendations to assist instructors and students. As the social context of teaching and learning changes within these new spaces, we need to reorient not only our pedagogical approach but also the social arrangements under which learning happens.

Note

1. The data collection instruments used in this study can be found online at http://z.umn.edu/lsr.

References

Amedeo, D., R. G. Golledge, and R. J. Stimson. 2009. *Person Environment Behavior Research: Investigating Activities and Experiences in Spaces and Environments*. New York, NY: Guilford.

Beichner, R. J., J. M. Saul, D. S. Abbott, J. J. Morse, D. L. Deardorff, R. J. Allain, and J. S. Risley. 2007. "Student-Centered Activities for Large Enrollment Undergraduate Programs (SCALE-UP) Project." In *Research-Based Reform of University Physics*, edited by E. Redish and P. Cooney, 1–42. College Park, MD: American Association of Physics Teachers.

Billson, J. M., and R. G. Tiberius. 1991. "Effective Social Arrangements for Teaching and Learning." In *College Teaching: From Theory to Practice*, New Directions for Teaching and Learning, no. 45, edited by R. J. Menges and M. Svinicki, 87–110. San Francisco, CA: Jossey-Bass.

Bordin, E. S. 1979. "The Generalizability of the Psychoanalytic Concept of the Working Alliance." *Psychotherapy: Theory, Research, and Practice* 16: 252–260. doi:10.1037/h0085885.

Bransford, J. D., A. L. Brown, and R. R. Cocking. 2000. *How People Learn*. Washington, DC: National Academy Press.

Brooks, D. C. 2011. "Space Matters: The Impact of Formal Learning Environments on Student Learning." *British Journal of Educational Technology* 42 (5): 719–726. doi:10.1111/j.1467-8535.2010.01098.x.

Brooks, D. C. 2012. "Space and Consequences: The Impact of Different Formal Learning Spaces on Instructor and Student Behavior." *Journal of Learning Spaces* 1. http://z.umn.edu/jols.

Chickering, A. W., and Z. F. Gamson, eds. 1991. *Applying the Seven Principles for Good Practice in Undergraduate Education*, New Directions for Teaching and Learning, no. 47. San Francisco: Jossey-Bass.

Dori, Y. J., and J. Belcher. 2005. "How Does Technology-Enabled Active Learning Affect Undergraduate Students' Understanding of Electromagnetism Concepts?" *Journal of the Learning Sciences* 14: 243–279. doi:10.1207/s15327809jls1402_3.

Endo, J. J., and R. L. Harpel. 1982. "The Effect of Student-Faculty Interaction on Students' Educational Outcomes." *Research in Higher Education* 16: 115–135. doi:10.1007/BF00973505.

Johnson, D. W., R. T. Johnson, and K. A. Smith. 2007. "The State of Cooperative Learning in Postsecondary and Professional Settings." *Educational Psychology Review* 19: 15–29. doi:10.1007/s10648-006-9038-8.

Meyers, S. A. 2008. "Working Alliances in College Classrooms." *Teaching of Psychology* 34: 29–32. doi:10.1080/00986280701818490.

Pascarella, E. T., and P. T. Terenzini. 2005. *How College Affects Students. Volume 2: A Third Decade of Research*. San Francisco, CA: Jossey-Bass.

Tiberius, R. G. 1993–1994. "The Why of Teacher/Student Relationships." *Teaching Excellence: Toward the Best in the Academy* 5 (8): 1–2.

Tiberius, R. G., and J. M. Billson. 1991. "The Social Context of Teaching and Learning." In *College Teaching: From Theory to Practice*, New Directions in Teaching and Learning, no. 45, edited by R. Menges and M. Svinicki, 67–86. San Francisco: Jossey-Bass.

Tichenor, V., and C. E. Hill. 1989. "A Comparison of Six Measures of the Working Alliance." *Psychotherapy* 26: 195–199. doi:10.1037/h0085419.

Tinto, V. 1997. "Classrooms as Communities: Exploring the Educational Character of Student Persistence." *Journal of Higher Education* 68: 599–623. doi:10.2307/2959965.

Walker, J. D., D. C. Brooks, and P. Baepler. 2011. "Pedagogy and Space: Empirical Research on New Learning Environments." *EDUCAUSE Quarterly* 34 (4). http://z.umn.edu/eq1.

Whiteside, A. W., D. C. Brooks, and J. D. Walker. 2010. "Making the Case for Space: Three Years of Empirical Research on Formal and Informal Learning Environments." *EDUCAUSE Quarterly* 33 (3). http://z.umn.edu/22m.

PAUL BAEPLER *is part of the research and evaluation team in Information Technology at the University of Minnesota.*

J. D. WALKER *is part of the research and evaluation team in Information Technology at the University of Minnesota.*

4

This chapter explores whether a new learning space, designed to be more like a café than a classroom, provides an environment that facilitates active and collaborative learning.

Coffeehouse as Classroom: Examination of a New Style of Active Learning Environment

Anastasia S. Morrone, Judith A. Ouimet, Greg Siering, Ian T. Arthur

Indiana University's newest experimental classroom, the "Collaboration Café," was designed to facilitate active and collaborative learning while also exploring a new classroom design that shares café-style characteristics. The room includes limestone accents, plentiful natural light, and brightly colored seating (Lei 2010). There are high and low bistro-style tables at the center, booths, and soft sofa seating clustered around small coffee tables (see Figures 4.1 and 4.2). The technology in the room includes multiple projection possibilities and collaborative tables that support the sharing of laptop images on video monitors, as well as access to six or more PCs and a networked printer, all to facilitate student engagement with course materials and each other. Unlike other active learning classrooms, the design of the Collaboration Café does not assume any particular pedagogical approach; rather, the space is intended to provide a flexible, technology-rich, collaborative space for faculty to use in whatever ways best enable them to achieve their instructional goals.

Why We Conducted the Study

The overarching goal of this study was to understand how instructors were using this experimental classroom and whether this new style of classroom provides an environment that facilitates active and collaborative learning.

Method

The following sections provide details regarding the subjects of this study, the research instruments used, and our data collection methods.

New Directions for Teaching and Learning, no. 137, Spring 2014 © 2014 Wiley Periodicals, Inc.
Published online in Wiley Online Library (wileyonlinelibrary.com) • DOI: 10.1002/tl.20084

41

Figure 4.1. Students Working at Their Tables on an Assignment

Source: Photograph by the Trustees of Indiana University.

Figure 4.2. Student Team Consulting with Their Professor

Source: Photograph by the Trustees of Indiana University.

Participants. During the fall 2012 semester, ten instructors taught fifteen classes in the Collaboration Café (Cedar Hall 102). The classes varied in both type and focus (that is, Introduction to International Studies, Telecommunications, Spanish Language Pedagogy, English, Statistics, Folklore, and History) and had a total of 372 students enrolled.

Instrument and Data Collection Description. Mixed methods research that meaningfully integrates qualitative and quantitative approaches can result in the enrichment of both data types and "provide stronger evidence for a conclusion through convergence and corroboration of findings" (Johnson and Onwuegbuzie 2004, 21). Video data, in particular, can serve as an effective means of exploring the validity of subjective accounts of learning and instruction activities (Jordan and Henderson 1995; Rosenstein 2002; Stigler, Gallimore, and Hiebert 2000). For these reasons, a "convergent parallel" mixed methods design (Creswell and Plano-Clark 2007) was chosen for this study, triangulating faculty reports of classroom behaviors with quantitative and qualitative survey assessments of student perceptions and surveillance video of actual classroom behaviors.

Daily Usage Checklist. This instrument was used to ascertain if the classroom environment helped faculty to accomplish their instructional goals, and asked what equipment they used and what was used by students during class.

Room Surveillance Video. Because the classroom serves as both a classroom and a Student Technology Center (STC), for security purposes, four surveillance cameras with fixed viewpoints were permanently installed. These cameras provided video-only observation data that were used for coding the classroom activity. A coding protocol was developed in iterative attempts to describe classroom behaviors and broadly characterize classroom interactions and technologies used. Observations made over the course of the fall 2012 semester were reviewed in order to assess the relative stability of patterns over time.

Student Survey. A quantitative and qualitative student survey that focused on classroom space and activities was sent to all 372 students who took a class in fall 2012 in the Collaboration Café. As an incentive, students were entered into a $50 Visa gift card drawing for completing the questionnaire, which yielded a 48 percent response rate. The usual gender bias occurred with a higher percentage of females (52 percent) responding than males (35 percent); however, students of color had a higher response rate (50 percent) than the white students (43 percent). Chi-square and mean tests were performed to see if there were differences by gender or race; however, no statistical significant differences were found (see Table 4.1).

Faculty Interviews. To obtain a richer understanding of faculty approaches to teaching in this space, and their retrospective perceptions, all instructors were invited to participate in interviews. Five faculty members agreed to share their experiences and were asked four questions, three of which were parallel to the items asked in the student survey.

NEW DIRECTIONS FOR TEACHING AND LEARNING • DOI: 10.1002/tl

Table 4.1. Student Responder Nonresponder Comparison by Demographics

	Nonresponder		Responder	
Gender				
Female	106	48%	116	52%
Male	98	65%	52	35%
Ethnicity				
White	148	57%	113	43%
Nonwhite	56	50%	55	50%
Total	204	55%	168	45%

1. Please describe one situation in which this room WORKED WELL for you. Provide as many details as possible.
2. Please describe one situation in which this room DID NOT WORK WELL for you. Please provide as many details as possible.
3. What are your overall thoughts about teaching in the Cedar Hall 102 classroom?
4. Please describe how your approach to designing class activities in CH 102 differed from how you typically have approached designing class activities in more traditional classrooms.

Key Findings

In this section, we report on our major findings regarding the impact of the space on faculty-student collaboration; the evaluation of the room design, furniture, comfort, and overall feel; and the use of technology in the room.

Faculty and Students Overwhelmingly Felt That the Space Was Conducive to Collaboration. Students reported high levels of student-faculty and student-student interaction. Approximately 70 percent reported interacting with the instructor during an in-class learning activity at least once a week, while 80 percent of respondents reported that the instructor consulted with groups of students during an in-class learning activity. A smaller percentage of students, 74 percent, reported that an in-class learning activity required students to explain course ideas or concepts to other students; however, 93 percent of responders agreed or strongly agreed that the space facilitates multiple types of learning activities, which is supported by the checklists, faculty interviews, and video.

In addition, 86 percent of students agreed or strongly agreed with the statement that the Collaboration Café makes it easier than a traditional classroom to collaborate with classmates. A smaller percentage of students, 67 percent, agreed or strongly agreed with the statement that they participated more than they do in a traditional classroom.

Students overwhelmingly felt that the space was conducive to group work and discussions. These were the most frequently cited modes of

interaction in survey open-ended questions, with the majority of participants making one or more explicit references to the enhancement or support of "groups, collaboration," and/or "discussion." Students also felt that
presentations and group presentations were well supported by the room.

Another enhanced form of interaction cited by students was peer-to-
peer social connecting (as opposed to strictly class-related interaction). Students reported feeling "more connected" and having a "better sense of community" than they would in traditional classrooms; however, a few students
reported feeling that discussions and social connectivity were negatively impacted by the space. In particular, the design of the room and the variety of
discrete learning spaces (that is, small tables and booths that orient students
toward one another) were seen to segregate the class into distinct subsets,
thus decreasing interactivity among the class as a whole.

Consistent with these findings, discussion was reported as the most
widely used instructional method; however, there were sometimes significant discrepancies with what we observed on the video. Specifically, some
faculty reported engaging in class-wide discussion, when observation of the
video indicated that the class was almost entirely lecture based, with only
brief and infrequent contributions from students. In addition, some faculty
reported that students shared work during class, but we were unable to find
any observable corresponding behavior on video, calling into question how
"sharing of work" was being interpreted.

Finally, even though the classroom was widely cited as lending itself to
collaborative activities, more than 50 percent of the responses to the daily
usage checklist indicate that faculty were using lecture during class, which
was corroborated by observations. We also observed many classes exhibit-
ing a general front-back orientation by virtue of the location of the large
projection screen and whiteboard surface on the west wall of the room, and
the nearby instructor lectern.

**Design of the Room and Furniture Received Mixed Reviews from
Faculty and Students.**   While 81 percent of the students reported that the
classroom environment was more conducive to learning than the traditional
classroom design, reviews of the size of the room were more ambivalent
than reviews of other qualities cited by students. For example, one student
who felt that the size of the room was problematic also said, "I liked it a
lot because I had more freedom to spread out my belongings/computers
and such." The classroom is 1,614 square feet and seats 49 students; using
standard university guidelines, a classroom of that size would typically seat
between 64 and 80 students. More often than not, the spaciousness was
seen as a benefit, but there were a number of students who evaluated the
size of the room negatively. One student shared that "during class, there
are times when the room is too large to adequately create an environment
of collaboration and community." Another negative evaluation addressed
problems an instructor sometimes had with hearing students in the large
space.

Table 4.2. Preferred Seating

	Rank 1	Rank 2	Rank 3	Rank 4	Rank 5	Rank 6
The soft cushioned chairs (either design)	44%	33%	15%	6%	1%	0%
The short tables	39%	38%	13%	7%	3%	0%
The tall tables	10%	17%	38%	8%	8%	19%
The computer desks along the wall	2%	3%	10%	38%	23%	24%
The booths with the computer monitors	1%	5%	12%	23%	43%	16%
The corner couch	2%	4%	13%	19%	21%	41%

A clear majority of students found the mobility and flexibility inherent in the design of the room to be beneficial. One student reported that "being able to move the tables and chairs around has made a HUGE difference in group work for my class that meets here. I participate a lot more because of this."

The generous space also allows instructors to create a variety of grouping arrangements. Instructors reported regularly creating groups of varying sizes—from multiple small groups of three or four students to circular whole-class configurations. Several faculty members pointed out that while their approach to using groups was not fundamentally different as compared with other classrooms, the qualities of mobility and flexibility inherent in the space meant that the implementation was much easier. Moreover, some instructors perceived that the quality of group work undertaken was better than what they observed in course sections they taught in other spaces.

The students were asked to rank order their seating preferences. Consistent with the findings above, the soft cushioned chairs and short tables were clearly preferred over the other furniture arrangements in the room (see Table 4.2), potentially for the ease in moving them around the room.

Instructor interaction with groups and/or individuals during designated group activity was also perceived to be enhanced by the physical characteristics of the room. Respondents noted that the spaciousness of the room and the ability of students to easily configure themselves into groups throughout the room allowed them to easily navigate among groups and join in small group discussions at the same "level" as the other participants. To highlight the significance of these points, one instructor noted that traditional classroom spaces make accessing groups difficult and require "towering" over students in a way that negatively impacts interactions. A few reports suggested that students did perceive this difference in the room. One student noted that the room "provides an atmosphere where our teacher can sit and talk with us in a more informal, equal (way)." Another noted that the room provides a "relaxed environment that makes it more comfortable to converse with the professor and other students." Other students also felt that the room enhanced group discussions with peers. One student noted that sitting at tables that automatically create groups "fosters a more comfortable environment for group discussion," while another said that the room "is much more casual, and turns a lecture into a conversation."

Faculty and Students Rated the Space Very Positively with Respect to the Comfort and Overall Feel of the Classroom. With few exceptions, students gave positive overall evaluations of their experiences in the room. When provided, the reasons for their positive feelings about the space were wide-ranging, but clearly, most students "like, love," or "enjoy" their time in the classroom.

Instructor-interview responses suggested that student comfort was an important contributor to making groups "work better" in the classroom. A significant number of students (approximately one-third of all respondents) made explicit references to feelings of comfort and/or relaxation, and thereby seemed to confirm that comfort positively impacted discussion activity. Interestingly, some responses addressing the comfortable nature of the space specifically made reference to reductions in stress and anxiety, noting that the space was "stress free" and that "the cozy atmosphere . . . takes the anxiety out" of class meetings.

Another finding that came to light in the student data that was not directly addressed in the instructor interviews was that "comfort" also had an impact on alertness, concentration, and/or the general level of activity in the room. Students claimed that the relaxed atmosphere "makes it easier to concentrate" and "keeps [them] awake." One student shared that the room "feels like a cross between a big living room and a classroom, which helps me focus." With respect to possible reasons for the space having an effect on alertness, several students made some reference to the novelty of the space, contrasting it with "traditional" classrooms and characterizing the overall design as "modern." Interestingly, one student noted that while she was very pleased with the space, her first encounter with the room was problematic. She said, "I walked in and didn't know what to do. I didn't know where to sit." The room seems to disrupt pre-existing schemas for what a classroom should be, thereby capturing students' attention.

The majority of references to the qualities of light in the room and to the windows, explicitly, were quite positive. Students reported that "the lighting is great," that they "love the lighting," and that "all of the natural light from the windows . . . makes the room feel more vibrant and keeps me alert." Multiple instructors noted their appreciation of the amount of natural light available in the room.

With the Exception of the Projector, the Technology in the Room Was Not Used to Significant Effect. On the open-ended items on the student survey, "technology" was primarily referenced in a generic, abstract way, and was evaluated very positively by students. Students perceived the space to be "very technologically advanced," and held it to be a valuable resource. When students did specify benefits of technology, or specific

Table 4.3. Student Reported Helpfulness of Technologies

Reflecting on the various technologies in the room, how helpful were these tools in learning the course material?

	Not Helpful	Somewhat Helpful	Helpful	Very Helpful
Projector	5%	3%	26%	66%
Interactive whiteboard	20%	16%	31%	34%
Portable whiteboards	30%	16%	27%	27%
Whiteboard camera	30%	21%	22%	26%
Computers in booths	31%	20%	22%	27%
Computers along wall	22%	14%	27%	37%

technologies, they were most often associated with visual displays (projectors and various whiteboards) and/or presentation activities. Students felt presentation activities were very well supported by the "technology" in the room. Mobile whiteboards used to present group work to the whole class were singled out for praise several times. These findings are generally consistent with what the students reported on the closed-ended survey question (see Table 4.3).

During video observations, use of projectors was clearly the dominant form of technology used. Interestingly, there was no observed use of the room's copy camera captured on video.

Also consistent with what was reported on the student survey and checklists, use of the interactive whiteboard was neither frequent nor consistent but was regularly used as a standard whiteboard and as a projection surface. Reports of interactive whiteboard use indicated that use was infrequent and that costs (in terms of the effort required to master the technology) outweighed perceived benefits. One instructor shared that, while an imperfect solution, it was easier to capture what was written on the board with a camera. During analysis of video data, both students and instructors were observed to occasionally use cameras to photograph whiteboards (including mobile whiteboards).

Looking across the courses, analysis of the video suggested that while patterns of technology use in specific courses remained stable across the semester, there were clear differences in technology use between instructors. For example, one course made regular use of mobile whiteboards while in another course, the instructor often used a document camera to project written text. Consistent with what the students reported and what was reported on the checklists, the dominant technologies observed in the classroom were projectors (most frequently projecting text) and whiteboards, in addition to mobile devices supplied by the students themselves (in the form of laptop computers and a variety of handheld devices).

Furthermore, the video indicated that mobile devices use appeared to serve both as an integrated part of class activity and as an impediment or alternative to class activity. In classes clearly utilizing group work, laptops frequently served as observable resources for those groups. By contrast, individuals and small groups could be observed to clearly "check out" of class activity with texting and other "incongruent" laptop use in some courses.

Finally, the interview data indicated that instructors felt that they had not been able to fully take advantage of available technologies, for a variety of reasons; however, they tended to perceive the available technologies as (missed) opportunities.

Faculty Development

Prior to the start of each semester, the Center for Innovative Teaching and Learning (CITL) and Classroom Technology Services offer orientation sessions for instructors scheduled to teach in the Collaboration Café. Because this room was designed to support and encourage collaborative learning in small- to mid-sized classes, rather than to significantly transform large-class pedagogies like SCALE-UP and TILE rooms (Van Horne et al. 2012), there is no requirement to attend the orientation sessions, although most instructors do participate in these sessions.

The CITL continues to search for effective faculty development approaches for this classroom that provide instructors with opportunities to learn about the room and to build a sense of community to share pedagogical experience among instructors. To accomplish this goal, a formal Faculty Learning Community (FLC) may be initiated to provide structure and incentive to explore best practices in the room and encourage collaborative Scholarship of Teaching and Learning projects. Video-based faculty spotlights may also be used to build a library of mini case studies about teaching in the Collaboration Café classroom.

Summary and Key Takeaways

The majority of the benefits of the room are associated with the nontraditional "café" atmosphere.

1. The spaciousness of the room was viewed as enhancing collaborative activities, but care needs to be taken to ensure that the space is not too large for the number of students in the class.
2. The abundance of natural light and comfortable seating was appreciated by faculty and students and viewed as making the environment more conducive to learning.
3. There were clear preferences for furniture that is easily movable rather than fixed furniture arrangements.
4. The technology in the room, while appreciated by students and faculty, was not used to a significant extent with the exception of the projector. There appears to be a clear "learning curve" regarding

technology utilization for the room, both for specific tools and for broader incorporation of technology, pedagogically.

The results of this study indicate that instructors using this room do not significantly change their teaching approaches; rather, the instructors who self-select to teach in this room typically are seeking a classroom environment that better supports their instructional practices.

Returning to the question of whether the design of the classroom provided a setting that enhanced teaching and learning, it seems that the answer is yes, but not without deliberate, intentional planning for different (nontraditional) kinds of interactions. Instructors who made the most effective use of the classroom had a plan for utilizing available features/technologies, as evidenced by a clearly structured sequence of interactions and technology uses being implemented on the first day of classes. In other words, there was an a priori intention, rather than a gradual evolution, regarding classroom utilization.

For the Collaboration Café, faculty development opportunities should continue to focus on support for exploratory teaching, rather than formal programs designed to promote large-scale pedagogical transformations.

References

Creswell, J. W., and V. L. Plano-Clark. 2007. *Designing and Conducting Mixed Methods Research*. Thousand Oaks, CA: Sage Publications.

Johnson, B., and A. J. Onwuegbuzie. 2004. "Mixed Methods Research: A Research Paradigm Whose Time Has Come." *Educational Researcher* 33 (7): 14–26.

Jordan, B., and A. Henderson. 1995. "Interaction Analysis: Foundations and Practice." *The Journal of the Learning Sciences* 4 (1): 39–103.

Lei, S. A. 2010. "Classroom Physical Design Influencing Student Learning and Evaluations of College Instructors: A Review of Literature." *Education* 131 (1): 128–134.

Rosenstein, B. 2002. "Video Use in Social Science Research and Program Evaluation." *International Journal of Qualitative Methods* 1 (3): 22–43.

Stigler, J. W., R. Gallimore, and J. Hiebert. 2000. "Using Video Surveys to Compare Classrooms and Teaching Across Cultures: Examples and Lessons From the TIMSS Video Studies." *Educational Psychologist* 35 (2): 87–100.

Van Horne, S., C. Murniati, J. Gaffney, and M. Jesse. 2012. "Promoting Active Learning in Technology-Infused TILE Classrooms at the University of Iowa." *Journal of Learning Spaces* 1 (2). http://libjournal.uncg.edu/ojs/index.php/jls/article/view/344/280.

Anastasia S. Morrone *is an associate vice president for learning technologies in the Office of the Vice President for IT and CIO at Indiana University and associate professor of educational psychology in the IU School of Education (Indianapolis).*

Judith A. Ouimet *is the assistant vice provost for curricular development and assessment at Indiana University.*

New Directions for Teaching and Learning • DOI: 10.1002/tl

GREG SIERING is the director of Indiana University's Center for Innovative Teaching and Learning.

IAN T. ARTHUR is a research assistant for University Information Technology Services (UITS) at Indiana University. He is also a PhD candidate majoring in counseling psychology and inquiry methodology in the IU School of Education (Bloomington).

NEW DIRECTIONS FOR TEACHING AND LEARNING • DOI: 10.1002/tl

This chapter reveals how thoughtful course redesign that specifically addresses the physical environment of a learning space can significantly improve student learning.

Pedagogy Matters, Too: The Impact of Adapting Teaching Approaches to Formal Learning Environments on Student Learning

D. Christopher Brooks, Catherine A. Solheim

Introduction

Building upon prior research conducted at the University of Minnesota, this chapter moves beyond the within semester quasi-experimental design that demonstrated previously that formal learning spaces can independently and significantly affect student learning (Brooks 2011; Cotner et al. 2013; Walker, Brooks, and Baepler 2011) and instructional behavior and classroom activities (Brooks 2012) to a longitudinal quasi-experimental design that isolates the impact of an intentional pedagogical shift that harnesses the affordances of a technologically enhanced classroom designed for active learning and team-based approaches to learning. Given that we know that space alters the behavior of actors and the activities that take place within them (Whiteside, Brooks, and Walker 2010), this line of research explores the impact on student learning that results from conforming one's approach to teaching to the formal learning spaces in which that teaching is conducted. Despite the lack of randomization of students to sections that would have rendered this project fully experimental, our results demonstrate that changes in one's approach to teaching to accommodate the space have positive and significant effects on student learning for all levels of abilities.

Literature Review

As in our previous research on learning spaces at the University of Minnesota,[1] we approached the question of how one's approach to

NEW DIRECTIONS FOR TEACHING AND LEARNING, no. 137, Spring 2014 © 2014 Wiley Periodicals, Inc.
Published online in Wiley Online Library (wileyonlinelibrary.com) • DOI: 10.1002/tl.20085

teaching in a particular space affects student learning with a quasi-experimental design. While the first study and its replication involved identical sections of the same course in the same semester by the same instructor with only the formal classrooms serving as the experimental treatments (Brooks 2011; Cotner et al. 2013; Walker, Brooks, and Baepler 2011), this study was longitudinal in its design, involving the same instructor teaching the same personal finance course in the same ALC one year apart with a faculty development program serving as the catalyst for a course redesign between iterations. That is, in this study, the room served as a constant and the instructor's approach to teaching the course was allowed to vary systematically. This design allowed us to isolate and compare the impact of deploying an active learning approach to teach in a space designed for active learning to a more traditional, lecture-based approach in the same space.

The basic structure of the project, which began in 2008, had the instructor teach the course in an ALC in a manner similar to how she had taught it previously in traditional classrooms designed for lecturing. Between the end of the fall 2008 and the onset of the fall 2009 semesters, the instructor transformed her approach to teaching the course from the one that relied heavily upon instructor-delivered content via lectures into a more student-centered active learning, team-based approach that took advantage of the physical and technological affordances of the ALC space (Prince 2004). The new course was taught in fall 2009 in the same ALC used for the fall 2008 version of the course. By structuring our quasi-experimental design in this way we were then able to test the aforementioned assumption about how changes to one's approach to a particular task within a particular space might change the outcomes.

Since the course (Family Social Science [FSoS] 3101: Personal and Family Finances) is a regular part of the major curriculum frequently rotated among instructors, the course transformation was limited necessarily. The course description, rationale, and objectives necessarily remained identical in both the fall 2008 and fall 2009 versions of the syllabus. The pedagogical changes implemented in fall 2009 included a team-learning approach that required class attendance, participation, and the complete review of all assigned readings, videos, and other materials *prior to class*. In addition to moving from a lecture- to a team-based learning approach, the instructor dispensed with a formal textbook and relied almost exclusively on internet-based resources (including the CMS) that could be accessed during class via the ALC's built-in technologies. Finally, the course assignments and distribution of grades were reworked to reflect the new emphasis on a team-based, active learning approach. All of the fall 2009 course assignments had analogs in fall 2008 with only one exception (the fall 2008 version had a midterm exam; the fall 2009 version did not), and while the distribution of points among them was altered significantly, the total possible points remained unchanged.

New Directions for Teaching and Learning • DOI: 10.1002/tl

Data

We collected data on 111 students enrolled in the fall 2008 version of the course and ninety-six students enrolled in the fall 2009 iteration. The preponderance of data was obtained using a survey instrument that focuses on students' perceived impact of the ALCs on their learning experiences, their evaluation of the features of the ALCs, and some basic demographic characteristics (http://z.umn.edu/sts). Respondents in each course were asked to complete the 45-item survey during the last class period of the semester in order to maximize the amount of student exposure to the ALC. Our survey data were supplemented with additional demographic and academic variables.

To assess the impact of the course transformation on student learning, the instructor provided disaggregated course grade data for students from each semester. For the fall 2008 section, grades were determined by three quizzes (twenty-five points each), in-class and on-line class participation (thirty points), a financial planner assignment (eighty points), two case studies (twenty points each), and a comprehensive final exam (seventy-five points) for a total of three hundred possible points. The fall 2009 section's grades comprised a midterm exam (sixty points), team-based class participation (twenty points), a financial planner assignment (eighty points), family case assignments (forty points), eight Rapid Assessment of Foundational Learning (RAFL) quizzes (adapted from Readiness Assessment Tests [RATs]; Michaelsen, Knight, and Fink 2004; forty points), and a final exam (sixty points) for a total of three hundred possible points. For ease of interpretation, we performed a linear transformation of all grade data into percentages.

Analysis

Since we could not randomly assign students to the control and treatment groups, our initial point of departure was necessarily an examination of the characteristics of the student populations in both sections to identify any systematic variation that might influence our results. We found that, despite the lack of randomization of subjects, the students in the fall 2008 course were demographically no different from the students in the fall 2009 course (see Table 5.1). These results further strengthened the controls of our quasi-experimental design by effectively precluding the attribution of any differences in outcomes to the latent demographic characteristics of the samples in question.

Our analysis of the impact of transforming the pedagogical approach to a course to accommodate the learning environment in which it is held began with a comparison of the final course grade expressed in terms of total points earned. Naturally, our null hypothesis was that there was no significant difference between the average grades earned by students in the

Table 5.1. Equivalency Tests for Demographic Variables, Fall 2008 versus Fall 2009

Variable	Fall 2008[†]	Fall 2009[†]	df	t-Score
Sex	0.200	0.211	198	−0.183
	(0.402)	(0.410)		
Age	21.362	21.379	198	−0.037
	(2.822)	(0.385)		
ACT composite	22.740	22.182	171	0.877
	(4.168)	(4.148)		
Metropolitan	0.760	0.732	144	0.381
	(0.430)	(0.446)		
Year				
Sophomore	0.109	0.109	144	−0.007
	(0.315)	(0.315)		
Junior	0.469	0.524	144	−0.664
	(0.503)	(0.502)		
Senior	0.422	0.366	144	0.685
	(0.498)	(0.485)		
Ethnicity				
White	0.721	0.674	197	0.726
	(0.451)	(0.471)		
Asian/Pacific Islander	0.144	0.190	197	−0.854
	(0.353)	(0.394)		
African American	0.096	0.116	197	−0.448
	(0.030)	(0.322)		
American Indian	0.029	0.021	197	0.349
	(0.168)	(0.144)		
Chicano(a)/Latino(a)	0.010	0.000	197	0.956
	(0.098)	(0.000)		

Notes: Sex: Female = 0, Male = 1; Metropolitan: Rural MN County = 0, Metro MN County = 1; Year and Ethnicity variables are dichotomous.
[†] Cell entries are means with standard deviations in parentheses.

two sections of the course. Students in the fall 2008 version of the course earned an average final grade of approximately 81.80 percent while students in the fall 2009 course earned an average of about 85.50 percent. This difference of 3.70 percentage points was highly significant ($p < .001$) and led us to reject our null hypothesis (see Table 5.2). Given our quasi-experimental design and the demographic equivalency of our student samples, this result suggested strongly that transforming the course to incorporate more active learning techniques and approaches that accommodate the affordances of the ALCs had a significantly positive impact on student learning as measured by course grades.

The adage that a rising tide lifts all ships is not necessarily a truism in educational research given that substantive changes in one's approach to teaching a course sometimes result in significant benefits for only one portion of the class, such as the lowest performing students. We therefore

Table 5.2. Difference-of-Means Tests for Aggregated Student Grades (Percentage), Fall 2008 Versus Fall 2009

Variable	Fall 2008[†]	Fall 2009[†]	df	t-Score	Normalized Gains[‡]
All students	81.801	85.497	194	−3.653***	20.31%
	(7.943)	(5.962)			
First quartile	70.989	77.854	48	−5.170****	23.66%
	(4.848)	(4.515)			
Second quartile	80.123	84.364	51	−9.110****	21.33%
	(1.873)	(1.486)			
Third quartile	85.587	88.514	44	−7.641****	20.31%
	(1.270)	(1.322)			
Fourth quartile	91.073	92.295	45	−2.196*	12.71%
	(1.993)	(1.796)			

[†]Cell entries are means with standard deviations in parentheses.
[‡]The normalized differences are calculated as follows: [(fall 2009 grade) − (fall 2008 grade)]/ [100 − (fall 2008 grade)] × 100.
*$p < .05$, ***$p < .001$, and ****$p < .0001$.

divided the students in each section into quartiles based on their final grades, and we found that the significant differences we observed in the aggregate also held for each grade quartile (see Table 5.2).

Given that the differences in final grade are significant within each of the four groups of students, we can conclude that the active learning approach employed to take advantage of the affordances of the ALC benefited all students in the fall 2009 course, not just the best or worst performing students. Certainly, the absolute differences between quartiles taper off as we move from the lowest to the highest quartile, but this is likely a statistical artifact of the ceiling on how many points a student can earn. That is, students at the lower end of the population have the most to gain, while students near the top have a more difficult task in making significant improvements as the limit of three hundred points or, in this case, 100 percent is approached. When we normalize the differences between the quartiles, however, we observe that the fall 2009 students demonstrated improvements of over 20 percent in each of the bottom three quartiles (and in the aggregate) while those in the top quartile gained about 13 percent over their peers. Thus, the improvements in learning appear to be distributed relatively evenly among the fall 2009 students.

An alternative possible explanation for the observed improvements in grades is related to the changes made to the assignments as part of the larger course overhaul. While we have normalized any variation in point distribution to a percentage scale, there may still have been differences in the form and function of assignments across the two sections of the course. With the exception of a midterm examination in the fall 2009 section, each version of the course possesses corollary assignments that can serve as the basis for comparison. Specifically, class participation, the financial planner

58   Active Learning Spaces

Table 5.3. Difference-of-Means Tests for Grades on Comparable Student Assignments (Percentage), Fall 2008 Versus Fall 2009

Variable	Fall 2008[†]	Fall 2009[†]	df	t-Score	Normalized Gains[‡]
Participation	82.071	96.667	194	−7.278****	81.41%
	(17.951)	(7.566)			
Financial planner	87.084	92.443	194	−3.624***	41.49%
	(11.708)	(8.564)			
Case studies	80.369	86.801	194	−3.654***	32.76%
	(15.782)	(6.577)			
Final exam	77.333	90.932	194	−9.882****	59.99%
	(8.337)	(10.867)			
Aggregated quiz assignments	81.972	91.284	194	−8.938****	51.65%
	(8.189)	(6.125)			

†Cell entries are means with standard deviations in parentheses.
‡The normalized differences are calculated as follows: [(fall 2009 grade) − (fall 2008 grade)]/ [100 − (fall 2008 grade)] × 100.
***$p < .001$ and ****$p < .0001$.

assignments, the case studies, and final exams are nearly identical; the three quizzes from fall 2008 and the RAFL quizzes from fall 2009 are comparable in the aggregate. If no significant differences are obtained with these comparisons, we must conclude that the midterm exam—the only assignment for which there is no direct comparison across sections—is responsible for essentially all of the variation in grades between the two versions of the course. Similarly, if a mixed set of results with some assignments gaining and others not is observed, we cannot rule out that substantive differences in the assignments themselves might serve as the explanatory factors. However, if the differences persist across all assignments, we must conclude, especially in light of the preceding evidence, that changes in the course resulting from the faculty development program are responsible for the improvements in student learning.

Of these scenarios, it is the latter that emerges from the data as we reject the null hypothesis of no difference in any of the assignment grades across the semesters (see Table 5.3). Students in the fall 2009 section earned significantly more points on participation (14.60 percent), the financial planner (5.36 percent), the case studies (6.43 percent), the final exam (13.60 percent), and the aggregated quiz assignments (9.31 percent) than students in the fall 2008 section. In addition to the confirmation that no particular assignment produced the observed improvements in grades, the sheer magnitude of the differences, especially the normalized ones, in assignment grades suggests that, if anything, the midterm exam served as a mitigating factor in the fall 2009 course. The mitigating impact of the midterm exam is confirmed with a test of normalized grades in which the midterm portion of the fall 2009 grade is excluded from the analysis. Without the midterm, students in fall 2009 section earned grades that are 9.40 percent higher ($p < .0001$) than fall 2008 students, a value that is approximately 5.70 percent greater than when the midterm grade is included (results not shown).

Given the controls afforded by our quasi-experimental design and the *de facto* equivalency of our student samples, our results suggest strongly that transforming one's course from a predominantly lecture-based format into the one that takes advantage of the formal learning environment of the ALC by incorporating active learning techniques has a positive and significant effect on student learning. However, it behooves us to consider the possibility of intervening factors that serve to mitigate or exacerbate the veracity of our conclusion. Fortunately, our data include measures of student satisfaction with characteristics of the formal learning space in which the course was held and student perceptions of the impact of that formal learning space on their learning experiences from both versions of the course in question. However, we fail to reject the null hypothesis of no difference for each of the fourteen individual measures of satisfaction with the environmental conditions, furniture, design, and other hardware (results not shown). In other words, we can confidently say that students' evaluation of the ALC did not contribute to the significant gains made by students in the fall 2009 section of the course.

Finally, we must consider differences in how students perceived the impact of the room and the activities in the room on their learning. We conducted difference-of-means tests for fourteen items designed to measure students' perceptions of the impact of the room on their levels of engagement with the instructor and peers, enrichment of their learning experiences, and flexibility of classroom activities offered and their evaluation of effectiveness of the instructor's use of the space and its technologies and the appropriateness of the course to the space. While perceptions of the impact of the ALC were slightly more positive for students in the fall 2009 course for each variable (results not shown), the only variable for which a statistically significant difference emerged is related to active participation. Students in the transformed fall 2009 agreed more strongly ($M = 2.893$, $SD = 0.792$) with the statement, "The classroom in which I am taking this course encourages my active participation," than students in the fall 2008 ($M = 2.609$, $SD = 0.902$), a difference that should be unsurprising given that the revised pedagogical approach specifically entailed active learning techniques ($t(146) = 2.032, p < .05$).

Conclusion

Until recently, the preponderance of research on formal learning spaces has failed to produce empirical evidence in support of the broad set of assumptions undergirding arguments advanced about the relationship of physical space to human behavior in an educational context. The evidence presented here advances the field one step further by demonstrating that instructors who modify their approach to teaching a course based on the physical environment in which it is conducted can improve significantly student learning across the board. When coupled with our previous findings that physical space has an independent, positive effect on student learning, these results provide support for at least three policy recommendations regarding space, teaching, and learning: (1) the construction of ALCs on college and university campuses is a worthwhile investment; (2) instructors teaching in these spaces should change their pedagogical approach when teaching in formal classrooms like the ALC; and (3) faculty development programs designed to support course redesign, pedagogical transformation, or technologically enhanced learning deserve either continued or increased institutional support.

Although the evidence continues to mount that both space *and* pedagogy matter when it comes to improving student learning, a veritable host of research questions remain unanswered. Some avenues of learning spaces research that might be worthy of future studies include, but are not limited to, the following: (1) replications of previous quasi-experimental designs, (2) investigations of the impact of ALCs from cross-disciplinary and cross-institutional perspectives, (3) comparisons of different active learning pedagogies in ALC-type spaces to identify the most effective approaches, (4) considerations of which features of ALCs are responsible for the observed gains, and (5) explorations into differences in the impact of ALCs on students possessing different demographic characteristics. Given the proliferation of technology enhanced learning spaces and the widespread interest in their impact in teaching and learning, answers to these and other questions will no doubt be forthcoming soon.

Note

1. The University of Minnesota's Active Learning Classrooms (ALCs) feature large, round tables that seat up to nine students and can be subdivided into three groups of three for team-based work. Additionally, the ALCs feature switchable laptop connections at each table that allows instructors to project content onto either a dedicated wall-mounted flat-screen display or a larger drop-down projection screen. Finally, ALCs have wall-mounted marker boards around the perimeter of the room that affords students easy access to a space on which to work. Additional information on ALCs can be found at the Office of Classroom Management's dedicated site to these innovative spaces: http://www.classroom.umn.edu/projects/alc.html.

References

Brooks, D. C. 2011. "Space Matters: The Impact of Formal Learning Environments on Student Learning." *British Journal of Educational Technology* 42 (5): 719–726.
Brooks, D. C. 2012. "Space and Consequences: The Impact of Different Formal Learning Spaces on Instructor and Student Behavior." *Journal of Learning Spaces* 1 (2). http://z.umn.edu/jols.

Cotner, S., J. Loper, J. D. Walker, and D. C. Brooks. 2013. "'It's Not You, It's the Room'—Are the High-Tech, Active Learning Classrooms Worth It?" *Journal of College Science Teaching* 42 (6): 82–88.

Michaelsen, L. K., A. B. Knight, and L. D. Fink. 2004. *Team-Based Learning: A Transformative Use of Small Groups in College Teaching.* Sterling, VA: Stylus.

Prince, M. 2004. "Does Active Learning Work? A Review of the Research." *Journal of Engineering Education* 93 (3): 223–231.

Walker, J. D., D. C. Brooks, and P. Baepler. 2011. "Pedagogy and Space: Empirical Research in New Learning Environments." *EDUCAUSE Quarterly* 34 (4). http://z.umn.edu/eq1.

Whiteside, A. L., D. C. Brooks, and J. D. Walker. 2010. "Making the Case for Space: Three Years of Empirical Research on Learning Environments." *EDUCAUSE Quarterly* 33 (3). http://z.umn.edu/22m.

D. CHRISTOPHER BROOKS is a senior research fellow for the Data, Research, and Analytics team at EDUCAUSE, where he conducts research on the impact of educational technologies in higher education.

CATHERINE A. SOLHEIM is an associate professor in the Department of Family Social Science, College of Education and Human Development, University of Minnesota.

NEW DIRECTIONS FOR TEACHING AND LEARNING • DOI: 10.1002/tl

6

This chapter provides practical strategies for addressing common challenges that arise for teachers in active learning classrooms. Our strategies come from instructors with experience teaching in these environments.

Strategies to Address Common Challenges When Teaching in an Active Learning Classroom

Christina I. Petersen, Kristen S. Gorman

Active learning classrooms (ALCs) provide opportunities for increased student engagement and interaction with classmates and the instructor. Reports indicate that students in these classrooms outperform their peers in traditional classrooms (Brooks 2011; Walker, Brooks, and Baepler 2011). In addition to these advantages, ALCs also present challenges for instructors who are used to teaching in more traditional classrooms and for students who are used to learning in these environments. In this chapter, we outline common teaching challenges in ALCs and provide strategies for overcoming them. These challenges and strategies come from the experiences of instructors we interact with in our work as teaching consultants and from our own experience teaching in ALCs. We begin with some background describing the differences between traditional classrooms and ALCs.

Differences between ALCs and Traditional Classrooms

A traditional classroom is designed with student seats facing forward with easy sightlines to a central focal point at the front of the room. A board, a projection screen, and an instructor podium are all located within these sightlines. Students ideally have unimpeded visual access to the instructor, the board, and the projection screen, and they are able to take notes on a desktop surface during the presentation of classroom material. This type of arrangement favors instructional approaches that involve transmission of information from the instructor to the students. It is possible to have student-student and student-instructor interactions in these classrooms, but the physical constraints of the seating present challenges in doing so.

NEW DIRECTIONS FOR TEACHING AND LEARNING, no. 137, Spring 2014 © 2014 Wiley Periodicals, Inc.
Published online in Wiley Online Library (wileyonlinelibrary.com) • DOI: 10.1002/tl.20086

In contrast, ALCs are designed to enhance small group student-student interaction and student-instructor interaction. Larger ALCs at the University of Minnesota seat 126 students at round tables, nine per table, with students facing each other. Multiple projection screens line the walls so that students at each table can view, and project to, a screen. The walls are also lined with whiteboards to allow students to record discussions with their tablemates. The instructor podium is usually situated in the middle of the room, which means that the instructor is unable to face all of the students at the same time. Also, most students are unable to view a projection screen and the instructor at the same time, and there is no central writing surface that all students can see.

The differences in physical layout between these two classrooms can present challenges for instructors and students who are new to these spaces. Common challenges tend to fall into two categories: (1) challenges due to the physical arrangement of the room and (2) changes in expectations about teaching as a result of the physical arrangement. We will address each category in turn, discuss more specific challenges in each category, and provide practical strategies for responding to each one.

Challenges Imposed by the Physical Layout of the Room

Here we discuss specific challenges imposed by ALCs due to the lack of a focal point, multiple distractions, and overwhelming technology. We suggest teaching modifications to address these challenges.

No Focal Point.   Probably the most impactful change from traditional classrooms is the loss of a central focal point with direct sightlines for all students. As described above, in contrast to traditional lecture halls with a board and a teaching podium in the front of the room, there is no single focal point of a front board for writing or showing visual material. Some students must physically turn to view a board or a screen and because of this may not be able to take notes on a desktop surface. It is difficult for the instructor to be seen by all students at the same time. Student feedback indicates that some students find this to be an inconvenience.

We recommend modifying activities that meet your learning outcomes and take advantage of the space. Because the space is not primarily designed to support transmission modes of teaching, we recommend using more active, group-based teaching approaches. For some instructors, this means modifying teaching approaches that rely solely on writing on a front board and lecturing. An economics instructor switched from writing on a board to using a document camera projected to all of the wall screens in the room. A chemistry instructor who likes to move around the classroom while teaching accomplishes this by projecting notes and slides to wall screens from an iPad. An engineering instructor solves an example problem on the document camera projected to all of the screens and then directs students to do another problem in small groups at their table.

When modifying activities for ALCs we encourage asking your students for feedback early in the semester to ensure that your changes are supporting your learning outcomes.

Multiple Distractions. Some students comment that the ALC environment is distracting. These distractions range from noisy small group conversations to easily being able to view the video screens of other students' laptops and electronic devices. Instructors also comment on the distraction of having to constantly keep moving to be able to see and make eye contact with all students.

We recommend directing student attention during class. To address some of these distractions, an instructor in higher education directs where her students should focus their attention. When moving from videos on the monitors to writing on a whiteboard, she provides direction in the form of verbal cues such as "Now I'd like you to direct your attention to the white board over here." To create periods of minimal distraction and to encourage student reflection on course material, she occasionally asks students to put down or temporarily close their electronic devices. This time is used for delivering critical course content, to give students a brief writing assignment, or ask them to contemplate a question she has just posed. She usually asks the room for silence during this period. This brief respite from distractions not only allows students to work individually and reflect, but also provides the instructor with a moment for reflection on how her class is going.

We recommend using folders to avoid the distraction of distributing and collecting student work, which can be challenging in a large ALC. Using folders keeps students focused on materials when you want them to and saves time. One instructor in biology has solved this problem by creating a folder for each small group. She fills folders before class with the materials students will need for that session and places them on the tables. As new materials are needed, she instructs students to withdraw them from the folder. She also uses the folders to collect student feedback or assignments at the end of the class session.

We recommend moving toward students engaged in distracted or distracting behavior. The configuration of the ALC allows for ease of instructor movement during class. An instructor in psychology uses this to her advantage by walking around the room so that she can identify students involved in distracted or distracting behavior. An easy first step she takes to address this is to simply stand near the student engaged in the undesired behavior. Often this action is enough to cause the student to stop. If she does need to address the student, the room configuration allows her to speak somewhat privately to the student while others work on a discussion question.

We recommend asking students for feedback early in the semester to determine if there are distractions that need to be minimized to support their learning.

NEW DIRECTIONS FOR TEACHING AND LEARNING • DOI: 10.1002/tl

Overwhelming Technology.   Some instructors describe feeling over-whelmed by the technology of the space. For some instructors, technology is present that they are not familiar with. Some feel pressure to learn to use all of the technology, employ it often in their teaching, and employ it well. Some students actually resent the breadth of technology, commenting that it is "overkill." Others feel that if all the technology in the room is not being used by the instructor then it is wasteful.

We recommend deciding up front what technology you will and won't use. This is a decision that should be made before the semester starts. To help with that determination, some instructors recommend observing someone else teaching in an ALC. Even sitting in on one class session provides you with a concrete experience for deciding how to interact with the technology in the room. Experienced ALC instructors also strongly recommend that you spend some time in the classroom practicing with laptops and equipment. An economics instructor echoes this advice as he recalled his first class in an ALC where he had trouble connecting his computer and lost fifteen minutes of class time.

After a period of observation and experimentation you may decide to forgo much of the technology in the room. If so, manage student expectations for the space by telling them what you will be using, what you won't be using, and why. Collect and respond to feedback early in the semester to gauge student reactions on how your use (or nonuse) of technology is impacting their learning.

Challenges Imposed by Changes in Teaching Roles

Differences in the physical layout and structure of a classroom precipitates changes to the way in which students and instructors behave in and experience the spaces in which they learn and teach. Here we discuss the specific challenges of the instructor no longer being the focal point, students being unable to hide, and potential loss of wider community. We suggest teaching modifications to address these challenges.

The Instructor Is No Longer the Focal Point.   As described in the previous section, ALCs are designed for students to be actively engaged with each other rather than centrally focused on an instructor lecturing. This can be an adjustment for instructors who are accustomed to, and may prefer, students looking primarily to them for a single response rather than asking students to engage with each other. One instructor found her first experience teaching in an ALC as a psychological adjustment for everyone involved. A chemistry instructor thinks about her interaction with her students in an ALC as closer to office hours or one-to-one interaction than a lecture. She explains that she knows it's better for the students, but it's difficult to switch from being the center of attention to just wandering around and answering questions.

New Directions for Teaching and Learning • DOI: 10.1002/tl

Some instructors also report discomfort with the loss of control they experience in turning over more of their class time to student group work. An instructor in psychology finds the experience as a little more nerve-wracking because she doesn't know exactly how it's going to go.

We recommend redesigning your course incrementally. Because of these changes in instructor roles, which can be substantial for instructors who previously only lectured, we suggest that you modify your courses in stages. One instructor states that she couldn't have handled preparing everything at once. She recommends making only a few changes to your course the first time you teach in an ALC and then assess what's working and what needs to be fixed before making more changes. Another instructor suggests taking "little sane steps" as you adjust your pedagogy. She recommends starting by inserting small formative assessments, like asking a conceptual question about the material just covered, as a way to gauge student understanding. As you become more comfortable with this, then it is easier to think about adding more involved activities and interaction. Another instructor began incrementally by simply having students work on some example problems in their groups rather than solving all of the problems for them, as he did in the lecture setting. Another simple change he made was turning rhetorical questions that he used to raise to the whole class into questions that students discuss at their tables. Another way to accomplish this is by making changes in stages. In the first stage, add more active learning approaches in a traditional classroom. In the next phase, move to an ALC employing these same active learning strategies. Once comfortable in an ALC, more active learning strategies can be added.

We are aware that some students are resistant to approaches that ask them to take more responsibility for their learning. Some students expect and prefer to be passive and have all the answers come from the instructor.

We recommend communicating your philosophy on teacher and student roles up front. We suggest that you manage student expectations by articulating what you believe your role as a teacher is in the ALC and the roles you expect your students to play in their learning. Importantly, tell them why you are taking this approach. Put this information in your syllabus, so students will know what to expect on the first day of class. One instructor informs students that she purposely chose an ALC to teach in because it offers advantages for their learning. She then enumerates what those advantages are (improved engagement and opportunities for small group teaching practice with feedback). She notes that some students may come into her class having negative experiences in an ALC in previous courses. She acknowledges to students up front that in addition to the advantages, the space also poses challenges to their learning and addresses this by informing students that she will be collecting their feedback about the classroom early in the semester so that she can make changes to better accommodate their learning.

Students Can't Hide.   We encourage the use of student groups in ALCs. Students working in groups experience increased social support, report higher satisfaction with their learning, and learn better than students working as individuals (Johnson, Johnson, and Smith 2007). One instructor recommends assigning groups as an important component of making the class work. In a large class, this allows student to get to know some of their classmates well. However, some students don't want to interact with either the instructor or their classmates and may prefer the passivity that is afforded by sitting in the back of a large lecture hall.

We recommend setting expectations for student-instructor and student-student interaction. Manage student expectations by articulating your expectations for class participation, interacting with peers, and interacting with you. Do this early, preferably on the first day of class, so that an alternate culture is not established. Questions to consider when you decide on your expectations include the following. Should students raise their hand and be recognized by you before speaking? Should students use the microphone when commenting or asking questions? Should students develop guidelines for respectful discussions on potentially hot-button issues? Also tell them why you have decided on your classroom expectations. Consider putting this information into your syllabus.

One instructor prevents students from hiding by using a cold call technique with a random name generator to keep all students attuned to his questions, but he takes advantage of the classroom configuration by allowing the called-upon student to confer with her tablemates before answering the question. Ask for and respond to early feedback to see how your approaches impact student learning.

Loss of Wider Community.   ALC instructors report many benefits of having students work in small groups. One downside, however, is that some students and instructors miss being able to hear from or interact with the entire class. An English instructor remarks that the room is tailor-made for small group discussion, but she struggles a bit with bringing everyone into the large group discussion.

We recommend setting aside time for large group interaction. Set aside time for large group reporting out to take advantage of the many voices that you have in the room. One instructor states that even though her students feel connected with their tablemates she also keeps discussion at the whole class level, which builds community throughout the room.

When doing large group discussion following a small group discussion, we recommend extending the discussion in the large group format so that it builds on the small group discussion rather than repeating it. For example, you might ask small groups to examine a graph showing the relationship between family size and the cost of living in various cities. If groups were able to identify the patterns in the graph, having groups report out their process for identifying the pattern in the graph could likely be skipped and the time could be used to discuss questions where there is more likely a divergence of opinion or experience, such as the implications of this finding or how it relates to the course themes.

You may consider going a step further and occasionally introduce activities that require students to interact with students from other tables. One instructor does this by asking students to count off to get into different groups for small group discussion. A biology instructor designs activities where small groups work together on an activity with similar, but slightly different foci (for instance the predictions for offspring from different genetic crosses), and then the groups rotate to the next table over so they can provide another group with feedback on their work. Feedback from students indicate that they appreciate an opportunity to get to know their classmates from outside of their group and hear others' perspectives on their work. With a nod to logistics, students appreciate advance warning of how long they will remain in their new groups so that they can decide which materials to bring with them. Ask for early feedback to see how your level of large group interaction impacts your students' learning.

Methods for Using Student Feedback to Address Challenges

A common thread that runs throughout these suggestions is to ask your students for feedback early in the semester while you still have time to make changes. One instructor asks her students on the first day of class: what do you think of this space given the kind of class this is? Together, she and her students agree to spend a week trying it out and then make adjustments for the rest of the semester. Another instructor collects feedback early in every semester on the space by asking students the following questions. What about this classroom helps your learning? What about this classroom hinders your learning? What change to this classroom would benefit your learning? She then shares the feedback with the entire class and either makes changes to accommodate student requests or explains why she won't make accommodations when it's not possible or appropriate, for instance when students ask for a change in the time the class meets. She reports that student complaints about the space decreased dramatically after she began using this approach.

In this chapter, we have provided several strategies for addressing common challenges when teaching in an ALC from instructors who use these spaces. Some of these strategies address instructor concerns and others address student concerns, but their ultimate goal is to improve student learning. Application of these strategies may need modification to fit your specific subject matter and student needs. We summarize these strategies in Table 6.1, categorizing them by when we suggest adapting them.

Before class, design activities that take advantage of the space but still meet your learning outcomes. If it is the first time you have used the space, we recommend an incremental approach that includes deciding which technology you will and won't use during the semester.

Table 6.1. Summary of Recommendations for Teaching in ALCs

Before Class Starts	First Day of Class	During Class Sessions
Design activities that meet your learning outcomes and take advantage of the space.	Communicate your philosophy about teacher and student roles.	Direct student attention during class.
Decide what technology you will and won't use.	Articulate expectations for student-instructor and student-student interaction.	Set aside time for large group interaction.
Take an incremental approach to changes in teaching.	Inform students that you will solicit their feedback.	Ask for student feedback early in the semester.

On the first day of class we recommend articulating to your students your rationale for choosing an ALC and how it will benefit their learning. Also communicate your expectations for their interactions with you and with each other. Advise students that you will solicit their feedback early in the semester to make adjustments as needed.

During the rest of the term, direct student attention to where you would like it verbally, with resource folders on tables, and by creating occasional quiet periods. Periodically set aside time for large group interaction and collect and respond to student feedback at least once during the semester. Use student feedback to make adjustments to your teaching and aid in your incremental planning before class in the next term.

References

Brooks, D. C. 2011. "Space Matters: The Impact of Formal Learning Environments on Student Learning." *British Journal of Educational Technology* 42 (5): 719–726.

Johnson, D. W., R. T. Johnson, and K. A. Smith. 2007. "The State of Cooperative Learning in Postsecondary and Professional Settings." *Educational Psychology Review* 19: 15–29.

Walker, J. D., D. C. Brooks, and P. Baepler. 2011. "Pedagogy and Space: Empirical Research on New Learning Environments." *EDUCAUSE Quarterly* 34 (4). http://z.umn.edu/eq1.

CHRISTINA I. PETERSEN *is an associate education specialist in the Center for Teaching and Learning at the University of Minnesota.*

KRISTEN S. GORMAN *is an assistant education specialist in the Center for Teaching and Learning at the University of Minnesota.*

A case study is described that examines the beliefs and practices of a university instructor who teaches regularly in an active learning classroom. His perspective provides insights into the pedagogical practices that drive his success in these learning spaces.

Conducting an Introductory Biology Course in an Active Learning Classroom: A Case Study of an Experienced Faculty Member

David Langley, S. Selcen Guzey

Introductory college biology courses are critical for attracting students to enroll in more biology courses and increase the quality of future Life Sciences researchers and educators (National Research Council 2003). Designing and teaching large introductory biology courses, however, is a challenging task. Many college faculty struggle with teaching introductory courses where students are expected to actively and intellectually engage in learning, develop attitudes toward science, improve writing and research skills, and become lifelong learners. Commonly voiced faculty concerns about implementing active learning strategies include lack of formal preparation for teaching, inadequate pedagogical skills, balancing diverse work responsibilities, and insufficient time and resources (Handelsman, Miller, and Pfund 2007). Even when faculty espouse beliefs that represent quality teaching, expressed conceptions are often incongruent with teaching practices (Norton et al. 2005).

The positive effects of using strategies such as interactive demonstrations, think-pair-share, inquiry-based labs, cooperative learning, case studies, and team projects on student learning and motivation have been documented (Cotner et al. 2013; Handelsman, Miller, and Pfund 2007). For example, Cotner et al. (2013) demonstrated "increases in student engagement and . . . average gains of nearly five percentage point in final grades" (86) of students who enrolled in an introductory biology course and met in an active learning classroom (ALC).

The purpose of this study is to examine the beliefs, experiences, and practices of one college faculty member who teaches an introductory

NEW DIRECTIONS FOR TEACHING AND LEARNING, no. 137, Spring 2014 © 2014 Wiley Periodicals, Inc.
Published online in Wiley Online Library (wileyonlinelibrary.com) • DOI: 10.1002/tl.20087

biology course in an ALC. We analyze in depth his process of preparation and implementation of the course and reconstruct it below, describing his perspective on teaching and outlining a host of insights for solid pedagogical practices in ALCs.

Study Overview

A qualitative case study was designed to uncover the practices of one experienced faculty member (pseudonym Daniel) at a large Midwestern research university. The university's Institutional Review Board approved the study, and the data were collected after informed consent was obtained. A case study approach was used since the study was an "empirical inquiry that investigates a contemporary phenomenon within its real-life context" (Yin 1994, 13).

A semi-structured interview protocol was used to conduct two-hour-long interviews that were audiotaped and transcribed verbatim. The first interview was conducted at the beginning of spring semester in 2012 to learn about Daniel's educational background, previous teaching experiences, and beliefs about teaching and student learning. The second interview was conducted in the middle of the semester to understand his pedagogical practices in ALCs and teaching plans for subsequent semesters in ALCs. In addition to the interviews, Daniel was observed four times during the semester. Detailed field notes were taken during the classroom observations. The case was developed based on analyzing the interviews and observations. Following a preliminary write-up of the Results section, Daniel read and approved the text for accuracy of our interpretation of his experiences as a teacher in ALCs.

Results

Daniel is a teaching associate professor (nontenure track) with a terminal degree in conservation biology and nearly twenty years of teaching in higher education as a faculty member. With a 14 credit per semester teaching load—much of it in introductory biology—he has "the luxury of being narrowly focused on teaching. And so it allows [me] to be innovative and to focus on the best approach to teach."

As the college began to construct a new foundations course for majors, the edict came down that all sections would be taught in ALCs. Tapped to teach with his associate dean, a nationally known educator and master teacher, "I went into it kicking and screaming. I was skeptical." Years of lecture-based teaching had cemented down the idea that if students weren't learning, it was their problem. "I finally got to the point," he said, "where I realized that's just a selfish perspective, it's an unwillingness to change and accept the evidence ... that [teaching in an ALC] benefits students."

NEW DIRECTIONS FOR TEACHING AND LEARNING • DOI: 10.1002/tl

Pedagogical Practices.   For students to function well as members of a team, a concerted effort is needed early in the semester to establish and reinforce good group habits. Not all students initially see this task as worthwhile, and Daniel recalled an incident in which a student interrupted his team teacher with the quip "Wait a minute. I thought this was a class about biology." The response from the team teacher was swift, cordial, but direct: "This isn't a class about biology. This is a class about being a biologist." The room grew quiet as the thought lingered for a moment. As Daniel recounts the incident, "Being a biologist is not just knowing biology. It's how to collaborate, to work together, because nobody works independently anymore."

If you followed Daniel around in the hour before class, you would not witness any preparation going on "because it's already happened. I typically have very structured activities that the students are going to be doing"— all of which has been prepared in the days prior to class. Student learning objectives, objects to be manipulated to nail down a point on DNA replication, and all handouts are ready to go from his previous class meeting. "I just kind of refresh…what we are doing today, what's the progression, what do I want," says Daniel. Even so, "there's constant tinkering with this stuff."

Students spend much of their time working in collaborative teams, discussing, debating, problem solving, using three-dimensional artifacts, or running simulations on the Internet depending on the problem. For Daniel, "the most important technology in the ALCs is the round tables. Everybody can interact with everybody else." While he has a set of guiding questions and key activities that comprise each class period, "you don't know where the students are going to take them…you have to be much more flexible in what you want to accomplish." The whiteboards are also keys to advancing and making student learning visible. As students work together to agree on answers to questions, the whiteboards "are an easy way for me to look around the room and see where everybody is at. It's pretty low tech, but it works really well."

Observation of one of his favorite lessons involved students working in cooperative learning groups to build an evolutionary tree for thirteen mammals. Students were given specific morphological, anatomical, behavioral, and habitat information and mined it to determine which information was useful for building the tree. Pictures of the mammals were placed on magnets, and with fourteen teams in the room, the whiteboards were filled with highly visible trees. Daniel reminded the students ahead of time that "every single [tree] is going to be wrong. And the students say, 'Why do you bother having us do this?'" The purpose of the exercise, however, was to have students at each table reconstruct their thinking process and explain that process to the larger class. He particularly enjoys this unit because "it forces them to come up with the thinking itself. And knowing they are going to get it wrong is actually liberating to the students."

NEW DIRECTIONS FOR TEACHING AND LEARNING • DOI: 10.1002/tl

Conventional resources such as workshops or on-site mentoring by his team teacher have been valued sources of his effectiveness as a teacher in the ALCs. But his fifteen colleagues who teach in ALCs are particularly influential, and they participate in an informal seminar every other week. "We have a very close working relationship. We share war stories...resources we've created...it's nice being embedded within a group of people that are all like-minded."

One of his teachers in behavioral ecology so heavily influenced him as an undergraduate student that she has remained a model to this day. What he gleaned from that experience was two key insights: "You need to be enthusiastic about the material; you need to show that you care about the learner. I think that perspective is probably the most important."

Team teaching is a regular fixture for instructors in the foundations course. Teaching with his associate dean has been mutually beneficial. "When I first started teaching with her," said Daniel, "I was frightened because her teaching style seemed so different from mine... [but] there have been convergences. I've become less structured...she's become more structured." Each week, one is the lead teacher, constructing activities, writing quizzes, and receiving feedback on content before and after class. They view their role as "coaches" but "one of the best things we do is challenge each other while the other one is teaching. We say to the students 'We're not agreeing. Welcome to science'...We're trying to give these students an authentic introduction to science."

Teaching regularly in the ALCs has convinced him that "if you give students the reason for doing something, they will do it...Most of your teaching...is having students do something...a lot [of what I do] is determined by what you see *not* working in the classroom." Although he gains much from his regular informal interactions with colleagues, students are the strongest influence on his adjustments as a teacher. As he states, "I take my cues from the students."

With a daily focus on expanding students' capacities as biologists, assessing those capabilities is an ongoing responsibility. First, "there's a lot of informal assessment of students. To me as an instructor, that's the most important part." Approximately 40 percent of the grade is based on work or projects accomplished as a team, but quizzes and formal exams also occur at regular checkpoints. The exams are important learning tools. "We have them do...a postexam analysis. They have to look at [their errors] and think about what happened. 'Why didn't you get the right answer?' We have them do that after every exam, so there is some learning that goes on in these big, high-stakes assessments that we have."

One signal task for the course is a major project that runs the final seven weeks. Students work in teams and write a research proposal in which genes are selected and used to solve a problem of social worth. Creating a unicorn is not an acceptable proposal; instead, students might focus on identifying a human or animal disease and propose a genetic modification to the organism to eradicate the disease. The proposal is delivered at a poster session on the last class period, and the teams seem to overachieve every year. As Daniel indicated, "We are generally amazed with every single project...we leave the posters up...[and] it is not uncommon for faculty to walk by and say 'What graduate course is talking about these things?' [The undergraduate students] don't get everything right. They're missing a lot of stuff, but they're getting a lot."

Insights.   After nearly seven years of teaching each semester in an ALC, Daniel believes he has become "much more comfortable with not being the authority figure in the classroom. I would never have gotten to that point...if I hadn't started interacting with students on an individual basis." His shift to instruction in an ALC coincided with a shift in his assumptions about student motivation and learning. "When I teach in the active learning classrooms," he says, "I realize how much I don't want to teach in the standard classroom. Teaching in a lecture auditorium ...allowed me as an instructor to blame the students for not understanding the material, because [I assumed] they're just not doing the work." The configuration and affordances of the ALC has provided the opportunity to reset his beliefs about students as learners:

> Ten years ago, I was saying, 85% of the students here at the university probably shouldn't be here because they don't want to be here. I don't believe that anymore, just because I've gotten to know these students as people, and they want to learn, they're willing to work hard, but you got to make it worth they're time ... I think every student here at the University is capable of amazing levels of learning.

Discussion

This study explored teaching experiences, beliefs, and pedagogical practices of an experienced university faculty member who has been teaching regularly in an ALC. While Daniel held predominantly teacher-centered beliefs early in his teaching career, his beliefs and practices shifted to a more learner-centered approach as he continued to teach in ALCs. Despite the caricature of faculty trotting out yellowed notes from one year to the next, research has demonstrated that pervasive change in faculty beliefs and practices is common across a wide career span (Beyer, Taylor, and Gillmore 2013), and Daniel is no exception. Co-teaching an introductory biology course in an ALC using active learning strategies was a critical opportunity for reshaping those practices.

ALCs enabled Daniel to use a variety of learning strategies. For example, round tables allowed him to implement team-based activities, and student laptop connections and microphones increased meaningful student interactions. Involvement in regular interactions helped Daniel's students feel that they are a part of a learning community, in particular, a community of budding scientists. In fact, Daniel and his colleagues have developed an undergraduate scientific community through the ALCs that rivals the considerable success of the Gateway Science Workshop Program outlined by Light and Micari (2013) at Northwestern University.

Our intention in this paper is not to portray an ideal approach to teaching effectively in ALCs. In particular, we note that the teaching "innovations" used by Daniel are pedagogically sound for standard classrooms as well. Good classroom teaching, regardless of the learning space, often rests on clear and organized instruction (Pascarella and Blaich 2013), empathy toward student needs, and directly and regularly addressing the rationale behind assignments and assessments (Fink 2003). Daniel's teaching perspective represents an informed and mature approach that leverages the affordances of ALCs. Rather than ascribe his capabilities to innate or "natural" processes, we assert that these teaching skills are learnable and can be used productively by college faculty for all learning spaces.

References

Beyer, C. H., E. Taylor, and G. M. Gillmore. 2013. *Inside the Undergraduate Teaching Experience: The University of Washington's Growth in Faculty Teaching Study*. Albany, NY: SUNY Press.

Cotner, S., J. Loper, J. D. Walker, and D. C. Brooks. 2013. "'It's Not You, It's the Room'— Are the High-Tech, Active Learning Classrooms Worth It?" *Journal of College Science Teaching* 42 (6): 82–88.

Fink, L. D. 2003. *Creating Significant Learning Experiences: An Integrated Approach to Designing College Courses*. San Francisco, CA: Jossey-Bass.

Handelsman, J., S. Miller, and C. Pfund. 2007. *Scientific Teaching*. New York, NY: W. H. Freeman and Company.

Light, G., and M. Micari. 2013. *Making Scientists: Six Principles for Effective College Teaching*. Cambridge, MA: Harvard University Press.

National Research Council. 2003. "Committee on Undergraduate Biology Education to Prepare Research Scientists for the 21st Century." *Bio2010: Transforming Undergraduate Education for Future Research Biologists*. Washington, DC: National Academies Press.

Norton, L., J. T. E. Richardson, J. Hartley, S. Newstead, and J. Mayes. 2005. "Teachers' Beliefs and Intentions Concerning Teaching in Higher Education." *Higher Education* 50 (4): 537–571.

Pascarella, E. T., and C. Blaich. 2013. "Lessons from the Wabash National Study of Liberal Arts Education." *Change* 45 (2): 6–15.

Yin, R. K. 1994. *Case Study Research: Design and Methods*, 2nd ed. Thousand Oaks, CA: Sage Publishing.

DAVID LANGLEY *is the director of the Center for Teaching and Learning at the University of Minnesota.*

S. SELCEN GUZEY is a research associate at the STEM Education Center at the University of Minnesota.

8

This chapter introduces a University of Iowa effort to enhance and support active learning pedagogies in technology-enhanced (TILE) classrooms and three elements that proved essential to the campus-wide adoption of those pedagogies. It then describes the impact of those professional development efforts on the curricula and cultures of three departments in the College of Liberal Arts & Sciences.

TILE at Iowa: Adoption and Adaptation

Jean C. Florman

Introduction

Thoughtful, effective teaching strategies are centrally important to the transformation of undergraduate student learning. While undergraduate student learning can occur in many settings and with the help of various facilitators, the heart of a university is the student/faculty[1] relationship and the educational experience that occurs within a course. Faculty members who effectively incorporate active learning pedagogies into their courses fundamentally change the classroom dynamic from one where the instructor is the deliverer of knowledge and the student is the passive recipient, to one where the instructor is a facilitator and guide for the students' active engagement with course content. Active learning pedagogies such as service learning and inquiry-guided learning (IGL) contextualize learning in authentic problems,[2] encourage collaborative effort and peer instruction, and challenge students to be more responsible for their own learning (Kuh 2008).

This chapter will describe the professional development provided to faculty members involved in an institutional project to encourage the implementation of active learning pedagogy as well as how that pedagogical shift created culture change within and even between several departments at the University of Iowa. Three elements stand out as essential to the broad success of the transformational changes brought about by TILE (Transform, Interact, Learn, Engage) at Iowa: leadership, communication, and collaboration.

Laying the Groundwork

In the 2009 spring semester, campus leaders at the University of Iowa began to envision an institution-wide project to develop technology-enhanced

NEW DIRECTIONS FOR TEACHING AND LEARNING, no. 137, Spring 2014 © 2014 Wiley Periodicals, Inc.
Published online in Wiley Online Library (wileyonlinelibrary.com) • DOI: 10.1002/tl.20088

classrooms. Modeled on the SCALE-UP prototype designed at North Carolina State University (Beichner 2008, 2013), Iowa's TILE classrooms were designed to encourage active, engaged learning. Each TILE classroom provides round, nine-person tables, three laptop computers per table (to encourage members of each three-person team to work collaboratively), an LCD screen for each table, wall-to-wall glass boards, and a "control station" that is centrally situated among the student tables.

The Office of the Provost created a Learning Spaces Executive Team (LSEC)[3] to generate space design ideas, free up funding, and manage access to the TILE classrooms. After considerable discussion, the team also recognized the critical importance of pedagogical training for faculty members who would be developing the new TILE courses and teaching them in the new TILE rooms. Thus, from the relatively early stages of the project, effective implementation of active learning pedagogies was considered vitally important to successful student learning in the TILE classrooms.

Staff members in the Center for Teaching (CfT) and Information Technology Services-Instructional Services (ITS-IS) began to design a systematic approach to faculty professional development that focused on pedagogies best suited for the TILE classrooms: inquiry-guided learning (Lee 2004), peer instruction (Mazur 1997), and in-class, team-based learning (Smith, Johnson, and Johnson 1991). SCALE-UP and similar models on other campuses offered clues about successful teaching strategies in physics and other STEM disciplines; we were convinced that the three pedagogical approaches in TILE classrooms would apply as well to the social sciences and humanities courses.

To broaden interest, we set the stage to interest faculty members in the TILE pedagogies and the new room designs. The Center for Teaching offered workshops on various aspects of student-centered teaching.[4] The Center and ITS-IS hosted two open conversations on TILE that brought together more than 100 faculty members from across collegiate boundaries to discuss the project, its implications for faculty teaching roles, and its potential impact on student learning. During one of these conversations, we "beamed in Bob"—a videoconference with SCALE-UP developer and Professor of Physics at North Carolina State University, Robert Beichner. As a professional peer and an active learning practitioner, Beichner was particularly adept at leveraging scholarly evidence and personal experience in response to faculty questions.

During two later events, we simulated the TILE experience for faculty members who gamely worked through simple inquiry-guided, team-based exercises related to the social sciences and humanities. They then graciously provided feedback about their experience as "students" as well as what kinds of professional support they would need to design and teach new TILE courses.[5]

Based on these experiences, we developed a three-day institute, which provided faculty participants an opportunity to immerse themselves in the principles and practice of the specific "TILE pedagogies," the time and resources to enhance their professional development, and a chance to forge new bonds with colleagues across disciplines and colleges.

The Institutes were copresented by visiting experts and CfT and ITS-IS staff. Bob Beichner led the first Institute (May 2010). The second and third Institutes (May 2011 and October 2012) were led by Jon Gaffney, who at the time was a physics postdoctoral researcher at the University of Kentucky. The fourth Institute was conducted solely by CfT and ITS-IS staff. Because a substantial number of faculty participants were in the social sciences and humanities, presenters provided non-STEM examples and exercises that especially resonated with those faculty members. And all but the first institute included two demonstrations by faculty members—one in STEM and the other in the social sciences or the humanities—who had already taught in the TILE classrooms.

The Institutes provided the theoretical grounding of inquiry-guided, team-based learning and a summary of the development of SCALE-UP at North Carolina State University. Using short lectures, video clips, and active learning strategies, we explored the nature of good teamwork and how to form, sustain, and assess effective teams; the power of learning as inquiry, the importance of creating strong learning objectives, and strategies for creating academically challenging questions that engage students in authentic learning; and the logistics of the classroom, including how to seamlessly incorporate technology (including whiteboards and clickers) and how to disengage from the control center and engage with the entire class.

Following the Institutes, faculty participants[6] were expected to incorporate the pedagogy and teach a new course three times during the next three years. During the course design phase, the TILE faculty fellows worked one-on-one with CfT staff and graduate students in ITS-IS. Faculty members also informally sought out their TILE colleagues with questions and offers to sit in on classes.

The four Institutes launched sixty faculty members into the world of TILE. Nevertheless, it became clear that faculty enthusiasm and scarce staff resources made problematic the likelihood of continuing multi-day Institutes. A new plan was developed to provide intensive, multi-hour training followed by periodic, topic-specific workshops. Since May 2012, the foundational sessions—TILE Essentials—have included the primary topics of the longer Institutes, albeit in a compressed format. "Essentials" are offered three times a year and fulfill the requirement that a faculty member must be "TILE-enabled" prior to scheduling a course in a TILE room.

TILE Accelerators are periodic, one-hour sessions that focus on specific areas of applied TILE practice, including enhanced technology training, learning assessment, and course transformation. Similar to the post-Institute period, instructors who participate in Accelerators can consult one-on-one with ITS-IS or CfT staff.

The new training format continues to draw interested faculty members. Nevertheless, central administration and collegiate leadership, open and frequent communication, and the best-laid professional development plans did not alone ensure a faculty welcome to teaching transformation. Collaboration with department chairs proved to be the critical fourth piece of the puzzle that ensured the broad adoption of these active learning pedagogies, acceptance of the redesigned, tech-infused classrooms, and creative adaptation of the TILE model.

Departmental Buy-In

From the earliest planning phases, we were convinced that Departmental Executive Officers (DEOs, or "chairs") would be invaluable contributors to the overall success of the TILE project. Staff members from the CfT and ITS-IS visited department chairs from six departments that teach a large number of undergraduate students. We discussed the benefits of student-centered, IGL teaching and outlined the project objectives and timetable, and we emphasized the importance of faculty pedagogical development and support and answered questions about how converting traditional classrooms to TILE classrooms would affect each department.

Department leaders appreciated being consulted and agreed to spread the word to other DEOs, a number of whom encouraged their own faculty to become involved in the TILE institutes. DEOs in Physics, Geoscience, Spanish and Portuguese, Biology, and Urban and Regional Planning participated in the three-day TILE institutes or the shorter TILE Essentials. While several of them actually incorporated the TILE pedagogies in their own courses, others participated in the training largely to learn about the approach and the technology, better understand how students would be learning in TILE courses, and consider how this provost- and college-sponsored project might play out in their departments.

DEOs proved crucial to the success of TILE in another respect. As sometimes happens when a new teaching idea is presented, some people on campus worried that departments would discourage new, untenured faculty from "taking the risk" to invest time in learning the "new" pedagogy and create courses that often require considerable prep time when compared to traditional lecture courses. To our delight, however, a number of DEOs and senior faculty encouraged their younger colleagues to participate in the TILE Institutes and create new TILE courses. One DEO expressed the rationale for this support thus: Why should a new faculty member get into the habit of teaching stand-and-deliver lectures and then have to relearn a more engaging, student-centered approach five years later once they have tenure?

In at least one case, a new assistant professor in biology was—in his words—"actually told to teach the TILE way" in his very first course at Iowa.[7] In addition, the biology DEO[8] provided crucial support by connecting new faculty members with experienced mentors and sending them to external faculty development opportunities, such as the Howard Hughes Medical Institutes hosted by the University of Wisconsin-Madison.[9]

The narrative of TILE in the Department of Physics and Astronomy likewise involved a supportive DEO who joined two physics faculty members in one of the three-day TILE Institutes.[10] The faculty members then collaborated to create and teach a TILE version of the lab sections for the introductory astronomy large-lecture courses. After they assessed the course as taught in the TILE classroom and decided that a slightly different classroom design would better suit the team-based, inquiry-guided approach for one of their lab courses, their DEO provided funding to purchase crescent-shaped tables for another classroom.[11]

Perhaps the most surprising case of a department embracing TILE occurred in the Department of Spanish and Portuguese. The narrative of TILE in Spanish and Portuguese was remarkable for several reasons: The pedagogy gained a foothold even before the first TILE Institute; it was rapidly adopted by a significant number of faculty members; and it was one of the first humanities departments at Iowa that became "TILE-enabled."

The DEO of Spanish and Portuguese[12] was an enthusiastic "fan," transforming the first of four courses even before the inaugural TILE Institute, and then continuing to advocate for the TILE pedagogies on campus and at conferences. Like early adopters in biology and physics, he welcomed UI colleagues to sit in on his classes, and although the courses were taught in Spanish, visitors nevertheless learned by watching him finesse the teaching technologies and roam the TILE classroom guiding student teams and challenging them to think more deeply about the course content. He notes that the TILE approach was "a pretty easy sell" in his department, whose faculty members were already attuned to new pedagogies and technologies for teaching foreign language, literature, and culture. Nevertheless, he helped ease faculty members' worry about risk by exercising the power of the purse with travel funds and research support to reward faculty members who took the initiative to engage with TILE.

Spanish and Portuguese was also distinguished by the fact that its successor DEO[13] also participated in one of the three-day TILE Institutes and proved to be a strong advocate of the pedagogy within her department and across campus. Thus, faculty members in the department—including early-career faculty—have benefited from the assurance that their efforts would be recognized and supported from one administration to the next— continuity that is essential when trying to encourage faculty members to take on a new teaching challenge. During the last three years across the dual tenures of these DEOs, eleven faculty members in Spanish and Portuguese have participated in the TILE pedagogical training, created new courses based on TILE principles and practices, and presented about their TILE experiences on campus and at national conferences.

Shifting Perspectives and Remaining Questions

A growing cadre of UI faculty members seeks pedagogical training and access to TILE rooms, and a number of them are now applying active learning TILE pedagogies in non-TILE rooms. More than a dozen TILE faculty fellows have volunteered to mentor their peers and demonstrated TILE exercises ("modules") at conferences and for local high school teachers, UI faculty members, deans, the UI Provost and President, members of the Iowa Board of Regents, and the Governor of Iowa.

Of course, not all faculty members choose this way to teach and the lecture approach also has benefits, including the ability to more efficiently reach large numbers of students and transfer more content knowledge. In addition, students often prefer modes of learning where they are not required to actively engage with their instructors or each other. To at least partially address potential student resistance (or at least bafflement) about TILE, Iowa faculty members have found it important to talk to students at the outset of the course about why they are meeting in such an "odd" room, what will be expected of them, and how it will enhance their ability to learn and practice the higher-order critical thinking skills they will be expected to implement throughout their lives. Thus, these courses begin by talking about learning and student responsibility—a thread that recurs as the courses unfold.

Not infrequently, Iowa faculty members and administrators discuss issues about the tipping point beyond which students might experience too many TILE courses, particularly if they are majors in a department that has a rich array of TILE courses. There is no doubt that inquiry-guided and team-based courses demand more of students—a willingness to accept and grapple with more uncertainty, to interact with other students and instructors, and often to invest more out-of-class time learning foundational knowledge. As the impact of TILE courses on departmental curricula begins to be felt at Iowa, continued conversation—and even scholarly examination—will begin to provide thoughtful, evidence-based ideas about curriculum design and development.

As faculty members continue to develop and apply TILE pedagogies at the University of Iowa, professional development for teaching assistants becomes increasingly important. Teaching the technology is relatively simple—the "switching station" is a touch screen that requires about fifteen minutes to divine. Understanding the philosophy and practice of inquiry-guided learning, peer instruction, and team-based learning, however, can mean a profound shift in attitudes about learning objectives, assessment, classroom management, and the very meaning of learning in higher education. In many courses, teaching assistants (TAs) are on the frontlines of interaction with students, and helping TAs understand the philosophy and purposes of active learning TILE courses will encourage their buy-in. When a disconnect occurs between the style of learning in a faculty-led TILE class and the style of interaction between TAs and students, undergraduates become confused about what is expected of them and how they are supposed to learn.

Training TAs in TILE pedagogies demands the investment of considerable resources, so several departments have developed creative ways to achieve their goals for TA development. A physics faculty member actively involves teaching assistants in the course design process so they learn how to create effective inquiry-guided, team-based, in-class exercises.

Two biology faculty members designed TILE exercises for TAs who teach the dry lab for "Foundations of Biology." The inquiry-guided learning, team-based dry lab exercises are fundamentally different from the "recipe" approach of the traditional lab experience. The faculty members meet weekly with the TAs to present the week's TILE exercises and how those should be implemented. Although time-intensive for the faculty members, this approach has been very successful and this model is now being considered by other departments.

In the future, the CfT and ITS-IS will develop a systematic training program for graduate students interested in the TILE approach. Additional discipline-specific application of these pedagogies could be provided by senior TAs in each department who have completed such training and taught in TILE classrooms. Departments also could offer one-semester graduate courses in TILE pedagogy as it relates to their own disciplinary needs.

As the University of Iowa and other campuses continue to implement the SCALE-UP model and make it their own, institutional and department leadership, broad and frequent communication, and boundary-breaking collaboration in the design and teaching of inquiry-guided, team-based courses will be essential in transforming student learning for a new century. Through the TILE Project, the words "transform, interact, learn, and engage" will continue to apply to faculty members as well as students.

Notes

1. For purposes of this chapter, "faculty" will refer to any instructor, whether tenured, tenure-track, adjunct, or instructional staff member.

2. Authentic learning "focuses on real-world, complex problems and their solutions…" (Lombardi 2007, 2).

3. The current team includes the Associate Provost for Undergraduate Education, CIO, Associate Dean of the College of Liberal Arts & Sciences, Director of the Center for Teaching, Senior Director of Information Technology Services-Instructional Services, Associate Director for Space Planning and Utilizations, Dean of Students, Associate Registrar, and Manager, Instructional Services.

4. Presenters have included: University of Minnesota (UMN) Center for Teaching and Learning Director David Langley (inquiry-guided learning), UMN Professor of Biology and Dean of the College of Biological Sciences Robyn Wright (the SCALE-UP model at Minnesota), Chancellor's Professor of Higher Education Emeritus at Indiana University Bloomington and NSSE founder George Kuh (high-impact practice), Vanderbilt Center for Teaching Director Derek Bruff (student response systems), Harvard's Balkanski Professor of Physics Eric Mazur (peer instruction, Big Data, and active learning), and UI Associate Professor of Chemistry Renee Cole (inquiry-guided learning and POGIL).

NEW DIRECTIONS FOR TEACHING AND LEARNING • DOI: 10.1002/tl

5. We specifically designed exercises not related to STEM disciplines since we wanted to broaden the impact beyond the sciences and math.

6. Because of their high visibility and institutional impact, the Institutes drew both faculty members who had previously worked with the CfT and IS as well as those who had not. Of the 112 faculty members who have participated in TILE professional development by spring 2013, 43 had previously been involved in more than one CfT-sponsored professional development event or at least one full-day teaching workshop, and 20 of those individuals had already participated in one or more multi-day faculty development Institute conducted in the years before the TILE project.

7. Assistant Professor of Biology Andrew Forbes.

8. DEO and Professor of Biology Bernd Fritzsch.

9. Following the redesign of the "Understanding Evolution" course as an inquiry-guided, team-based course, enrollment has increased each year, from 27 to 48 to 62 students, a phenomenon that also occurred in other biology courses taught with TILE pedagogies, including "Fundamental Genetics."

10. DEO and Professor of Physics Mary Hall Reno, Professor of Physics Robert Mutel, and Associate Professor of Physics Cornelia Lang.

11. The success of the astronomy lab project spurred one of the faculty members—Lang—to pursue another teaching challenge and develop a two-semester TILE course that she sometimes facetiously describes as "tracing the origins of everything" from the Big Bang through the "primordial soup" and the evolution of living organisms, ending with the rise of early hominids. This "Big Idea" inquiry-guided course will be collaboratively developed and taught by TILE-trained faculty members (and one DEO) in five departments: Physics and Astronomy, Chemistry, Biology, Geoscience, and Anthropology. The shared perspective of teaching inquiry-guided, team-based courses in TILE classrooms has enabled the seven faculty members to effectively collaborate to create and teach this rich and multifaceted course. Lang's creative efforts to apply and enhance inquiry-guided, team-based learning were recognized by a Provost's Office Student Success Grant and the President and Provost Award for Teaching Excellence.

12. DEO and Professor of Spanish and Portuguese Tom Lewis.

13. Professor of Spanish and Portuguese Mercedes Nino-Murcia.

References

Beichner, R. J. 2008. *The SCALE-UP Project: A Student-Centered, Active Learning Environment for Undergraduate Programs.* Invited white paper for the National Academy of Sciences, September 2008.

Beichner, R. J. 2013. *7 Things You Should Know About Collaborative Learning Spaces.* Educause Learning Initiative. https://net.educause.edu/ir/library/pdf/ELI7092.pdf.

Kuh, G. 2008. *High-Impact Educational Practice: What They Are, Who Has Access to Them, and Why it Matters.* Washington, DC: The Association of American Colleges and Universities.

Lee, V. 2004. *Teaching and Learning Through Inquiry: A Guidebook for Institutions and Instructors.* Sterling, VA: Stylus.

Lombardi, M. M. 2007. "Authentic Learning for the 21st Century: An Overview." *Educause Learning Initiative* 1: 1–12.

Mazur, E. 1997. *Peer Instruction: A User's Manual.* Upper Saddle River, NJ: Prentice-Hall.

Smith, K. A., D. W. Johnson, and R. T. Johnson. 1991. *Cooperative Learning: Increasing College Faculty Instructional Productivity.* ASHE-ERIC Reports on Higher Education. Washington, DC: The George Washington University, School of Education and Human Development.

JEAN C. FLORMAN is the director of the University of Iowa Center for Teaching.

*This chapter describes the processes and pedagogies used by one
school in transitioning from lecture halls to collaborative learning
environments*

9

Active Learning Environments in Nursing Education: The Experience of the University of Wisconsin-Madison School of Nursing

Beth Fahlberg, Elizabeth Rice, Rebecca Muehrer, Danielle Brey

Traditional nursing programs include classroom, lab, and clinical experiences. In the classroom, students are tasked with learning large amounts of content often through the use of PowerPoint lectures. In the lab environment, emphasis is placed on skill acquisition. During clinical placement in health care agencies, students apply knowledge learned in the classroom and lab in caring for patients. In recent years, this model of delivering nursing education has been challenged. The Carnegie Foundation National Study of Nursing Education found that the current models of nursing education do not adequately prepare students for the complexities of professional nursing practice (Benner et al. 2009). The authors recommended "sweeping changes in the pedagogies and curricular structures of nursing education... Classroom teachers must step out from behind the screen full of slides and engage students in clinic-like learning experiences that ask them to learn to use knowledge and practice thinking in changing situations" (13–14).

The University of Wisconsin-Madison School of Nursing (UW-Madison SoN) is responding to this call by redesigning learning environments and expanding teaching pedagogies. The goal is to better prepare our graduates for the current and future health care environments. This chapter describes the efforts of faculty at UW-Madison SoN to transition classroom space and teaching pedagogies.

Background

The UW-Madison SoN grants three degrees including a Bachelor of Science (BS), a Doctor of Nursing Practice (DNP), and a Doctor of Philosophy

New Directions for Teaching and Learning, no. 137, Spring 2014 © 2014 Wiley Periodicals, Inc.
Published online in Wiley Online Library (wileyonlinelibrary.com) • DOI: 10.1002/tl.20089

85

(PhD) in Nursing. The BS and DNP programs require students to integrate knowledge and skills learned in the classroom and clinical learning environments. The integration has been challenging for at least two reasons. The first was an over-reliance on a transactional style of teaching that disseminates information but limits opportunities for students to actively engage with the course content and each other. Secondly, our inflexible stadium-style seating in lecture halls restricted discussions and professor-student interactions.

To address the first challenge, the SoN has received funding for faculty development and course revisions through the Madison Initiative for Undergraduates (MIU). In accordance with the recommendations from the Carnegie study, some members of the faculty have begun to change their classes from primarily lecture to student group discussions and problem-solving activities that promote critical discourse. To address the second challenge, we are in the process of changing from lecture halls to SCALE-UP (Student-Centered Active Learning Environment with Upside-down Pedagogies) classroom collaborative learning environments using tenets of the SCALE-UP model (Beichner et al. 2007). A 72-seat prototype SCALE-UP classroom has been used since 2011, allowing faculty to pilot new teaching and learning strategies. Experiences with this prototype are informing faculty and staff as they prepare for larger SCALE-UP classrooms in the new SoN building, scheduled to open in Fall 2014 (see Table 9.1).

Faculty Teaching and Evaluation in the SCALE-UP Classrooms

Three faculty members were early adopters of classroom changes. Each revised her course to reduce the time spent on lectures and to support small group discussions and assignments tailored to engage student thinking. The prototype SCALE-UP classroom was used for these classes. Two faculty members used an incremental approach to gradually revise their courses and one faculty revised her entire course at once. All three used tenets from the team-based learning (TBL) model to guide their course revisions (Michaelsen and Sweet 2011). The TBL model includes four essential elements. The first is that student groups be properly formed and managed; student groups must be diverse, permanent, and the instructor needs to thoughtfully design each. The second element is student accountability. Faculty must create opportunities for students to demonstrate they have engaged with the course content, both individually and within their groups. The third element is timely and relevant feedback by the instructor. Students need input and direction from the instructor at regular intervals in the course. The final, and most important, TBL essential is assignment design: assignments need to foster and promote learning as well as group development (Michaelsen and Sweet 2011).

SoN faculty evaluated student learning gains in these courses using both informal and formal methods. Informally, students and faculty

NEW DIRECTIONS FOR TEACHING AND LEARNING • DOI: 10.1002/tl

Table 9.1. SoN Timeline and Accomplishments, Implementing Team-Based Learning in a SCALE-UP Classroom

2010–2011 preparation	• Gathered information about SCALE-UP classroom models and visited other universities • Applied for funding to support faculty development, fall-spring • Planned and constructed a 72-seat SCALE-UP prototype SCALE-UP classroom • Formed SCALE-UP classroom implementation team: four faculty, three academic technology staff • Attended Learning Environments Conference, summer • Used TBL model to revise courses for initial classroom pilot, summer
2011–2012 (year 1)	• Created online library of teaching resources on learning management platform • Held informational sessions, workshops, and discussions about TBL and the use of the SCALE-UP classroom • Taught first classes in SCALE-UP classroom, September • Implementation team presented pilot experiences to SoN faculty, January • Revised technological capabilities in classroom to better meet student and faculty needs.
2012–2013 (year 2)	• Finalized plans for Cooper Hall SCALE-UP classrooms, fall • Refined SCALE-UP classroom pedagogies based on student and faculty feedback and research • More SoN faculty revised their courses and began using the SCALE-UP classroom. Almost all undergraduate courses were revised by the end of this year. • Disseminated SoN experiences across campus using symposia, online resource sites, and social media • Formed a campus-wide Active Learning Community of Practice with regularly scheduled events • Informal groups of health sciences faculty and staff began collaborating on specific projects to use innovative application-based learning approaches in their own courses, including interactive case scenarios and interprofessional mock-code simulation experiences
2013–2014 (projected)	• Opening of new SoN building (summer) • Hold faculty workshops about teaching in the new 170-seat SCALE-UP classrooms • Teach first classes in new SCALE-UP classrooms, refining technologies and pedagogies based on experiences in this new environment (fall)

completed surveys, group discussions, and course evaluations. Formally, two small pilot studies of SCALE-UP classroom classes were completed using both qualitative and quantitative methods to evaluate students' learning gains, attitudes, and satisfaction with their class experiences. In the following sections, three of the authors offer first-person accounts of their experiences in transforming their courses to accommodate the SCALE-UP classrooms for undergraduate and graduate SoN students.

Reflections on Experiences with Undergraduate Students: Rebecca Meuhrer. I used an incremental approach to revise a required adult health and illness course taken by students in their second semester of nursing school. This course had been traditionally taught using lecture with little student, professor, and guest lecturer interaction and few chances for students to apply content. To begin to address these problems, I integrated small group discussions for four units including respiratory, diabetes, cancer, and orthopedics. These units were chosen because they had been taught as lectures over two class periods. The units were modified so students were expected to learn the content independently through readings, online lectures, and an online quiz, reducing the time in class from two periods to one. Small group discussions were also integrated during four other class sessions including concepts of acid/base and blood gases, patient communication, prioritization, and pharmacology. For these four classes, students were assigned readings and/or short online lectures to prepare for class.

Students were randomly assigned to groups of eight or nine at the beginning of the semester. When students came to class they engaged with their groups in an activity such as a case study or a patient problem. For example, during the respiratory unit groups were given two case studies to complete; one pertaining to a person with pneumonia and one pertaining to an individual with asthma. For each case study, groups answered questions related to assessment, diagnosis, plan of care, medications to administer, and patient teaching. While the group worked on the case study, students could ask questions about the content and discuss areas of disagreement. After the groups finished discussing the case studies, the class came together to discuss answers. Each group was randomly assigned to report back on at least two questions. During the discussions, students talked about areas of disagreement and material they found confusing.

Student reactions to discussions in the SCALE-UP classroom have been positive. Several students noted that the case studies and problems helped them think through and apply the content being presented. Other students felt it helped with critical thinking skills and promoted communication and teamwork. Still others thought it helped them better retain information. Students had two negative reactions toward the course redesign: a perceived lack of time to complete the activities and a dislike of watching online lectures outside of class. Other students preferred listening to lectures rather than working in groups. To address the negative comments, online lectures were shortened and presented as smaller topics. In the future, online lectures will be made more interactive by adding questions and links to information. It is not currently possible to address the issue of students needing more time due to the limited seating capacity in the SCALE-UP classroom prototype. The course is normally scheduled for about two hours in the classroom. On days we are using the SCALE-UP prototype I had to divide the class into two one-hour segments

NEW DIRECTIONS FOR TEACHING AND LEARNING • DOI: 10.1002/tl

to accommodate all students. However, the issue will be rectified as we move into a building with rooms that can accommodate the entire class.

Overall, I have valued the pedagogical changes. I have noticed three major positive changes in the classroom. The first is that there are more interactions among students and between the students and the professor. The second is my ability to identify concepts students have trouble understanding. By having students take part in the small group discussions, I can more quickly identify challenging issues and provide immediate clarification. The third is the opportunities for students to apply the content and take ownership for their learning. As an instructor, I have had two major challenges with the pedagogy change. The first is giving up the need to "get through the content." Students have to be trusted to learn the content on their own and I have had to give up some control about when and how this was accomplished. The second is the time it takes initially to change the structure of the class. Classroom activities need to be carefully scaffolded so the objectives of the course and unit are being covered in a meaningful way consistent with the TBL model.

Reflections on Experiences with Undergraduate Students: Beth Fahlberg.   The last two years I have led the implementation of SCALE-UP classrooms and TBL in the SoN. I was new to the SoN, with a background in nursing education, research, and teaching with new and emerging instructional technologies. Teaching in the SCALE-UP classroom helped me connect with colleagues in the SoN and other departments. The enthusiasm for teaching and learning at UW-Madison has provided the impetus to develop a community of practice focused on promoting collaboration and knowledge development in new teaching pedagogies and environments.

In the fall of year one (see Table 9.1), I taught the senior undergraduate Gerontology Nursing course and applied the TBL model. I taught this class in the lecture hall because of the 130-student enrollment using the 72-seat SCALE-UP classroom periodically for student group work. In my second year, I divided students into two sections so I could use the SCALE-UP classroom to examine the influence of the environment on the class experience. A survey I conducted of students in both years showed that the SCALE-UP classroom was a better fit for interactive learning among student groups compared to the lecture hall environment, and it provided a more flexible learning space. One student reported, "The [SCALE-UP classroom] worked well for group work and discussion of specific topics ... [It] is poor for lectures, as some seats face the wrong way to see the screens."

Many of our undergraduate students enter nursing school with learning habits that have been successful for them. They are often comfortable listening to face-to-face lectures with little active engagement with other students in class. Students then memorize the information presented and are tested on it. In contrast, TBL requires students to employ independent learning habits, personal disciplines, and time-management skills, both inside and outside the classroom. One student in my course said, "I did not think the active learning style helped my learning at all. For my whole college career I've been listening to lectures. This is what I'm used to and I've developed my own study habits and procedures for learning the material in this fashion." Students' previous educational experiences may have not prepared them for the high level of autonomous preparation that is required in SCALE-UP classrooms.

Other students exhibited an appreciation for TBL and small group engagement in the SCALE-UP classroom. Many students enjoyed the challenges of working with others and constructing answers to complicated questions. These students also appreciated the application-based learning opportunities in the classroom and may be more likely to understand that the problems and communication strategies they developed in their small groups would benefit them when they transitioned to the clinical environment.

Reflections on Experiences with Graduate Students: Elizabeth Rice.   Graduate education has evolved significantly over the last ten years. Novel degree programs, innovative teaching modalities, and the changing needs of a new generation of nursing students have inspired faculty to change their pedagogical practices. The initiation of a new DNP graduate degree program in the SoN prompted faculty to develop a curriculum "blending" both online and in-person classes to integrate the strengths of face-to-face learning and online learning to address educational goals (Garrison and Vaughan 2008). The DNP program educates students to become leaders in complex, technologically advanced health care settings. This necessitates ongoing opportunities to demonstrate their ability to practice decision making, solve complex problems, and demonstrate leadership within a group.

Using the SCALE-UP classroom prototype, I implemented a blended-learning format in the U.S. health policy course that is required of our graduate students. Graduate classes have traditionally been taught with professor-led seminars and pre-assigned readings and assignments. This re-designed course included five in-person classes in the SCALE-UP classroom and nine online classes focusing upon readings, films, and short lectures that pertained to specific in health policy topics. Students were assigned to small groups (five to seven members) which were maintained throughout the semester in both online and in-person classes. The face-to-face class components focused on challenging group application activities, such as policy debates, problem-based leadership scenarios, and case studies. During the last hour of class, student groups summarized and presented their work among the larger class with instructor feedback.

To gain a better understanding of the student perspective as it relates to the SCALE-UP classroom, a pilot study was conducted to describe students' learning gains, attitudes, and satisfaction with an active learning class experience. Students participated in one semi-structured interview and shared their perspective of the SCALE-UP classroom learning environment.

Overall, graduate students reported positive learning experiences in the SCALE-UP classroom prototype. The opportunity to share their clinical experiences with their classmates and learn from each other was viewed as valuable and effective. Through the group discussions and assignments, students were able to successfully connect broader health policy issues with their own experiences in clinical practice. This connection between policy and direct patient care enhanced their interest in the topic and realization that health policy is highly relevant for nurses: "I do think that being able to participate in discussion among classmates was really helpful. It engaged my own thinking more. And hearing people's stories and examples from real life...I think this deepened my learning."

Recommendations from students included their belief that classroom technologies should not be the primary focus in the SCALE-UP classroom, but making connections between their learning from the assigned readings and the class discussions was crucial as one student noted: "I feel like the policy [course] was more about doing the readings, thinking about them critically, and talking about it." I learned from my students that too often we are focused on the newest technology to enhance our teaching. For students, using technology was not the key ingredient of the SCALE-UP classroom.

As an instructor I learned a great deal about teaching using the SCALE-UP classroom environment and was encouraged by the enthusiasm and critical thinking exhibited by students. Because graduate students are familiar with the preparation needed to succeed in a seminar environment, my students were generally well-prepared for class and contributed to their small group discussions.

It was challenging to carve out a role for myself in this new learning environment. Knowing when to join student group discussions was one issue I had not anticipated as problematic, but I found myself reluctant at times to interrupt the lively conversations among groups. Developing my role as course facilitator, rather than director, required growing comfortable with allowing students to direct the discussion. Providing support and guidance for conflict resolution added some anxiety for in-class sessions because these types of occurrences, while fairly common, could not be predicted.

Designing interactive assignments that combined the TBL goals to foster learning as well as enhance group development took more preparation time compared to individual assignments such as papers. In the two semesters I have taught this course in the SCALE-UP classroom, I have closely monitored which assignments have generated livelier group discussions and more in-depth learning. Topics that are timely such as mandatory immunization or taxation of unhealthy food and drink were particularly engaging for students. They were able to link their clinical experiences of attempting to teach patients healthy behavioral choices with the most recent data on the inherent difficulties of behavioral change and motivation. For many graduate students, I have found that their learning is enhanced through development of connections between the course content and clinical experiences.

Summary: Lessons Learned

The challenges of teaching in a SCALE-UP classroom have provided us with an improved understanding of how both graduate and undergraduate students learn. Preparing students for the changes they will experience in their curriculum and garnering student acceptance of these changes is more important than we had originally expected. We discovered that students require ongoing support and clear information regarding the potential benefits derived from the SCALE-UP classroom learning environment. Our undergraduate students, in particular, seemed more comfortable with lecture-style classes where they listened to lectures, often with little class participation. Many are not used to the higher level of preparation that is needed to apply the content to specific clinical problems. We continue to develop methods of communicating with students how varied methods of instruction may enhance their nursing practice in the future.

Group learning and peer accountability was also a challenge for our undergraduate students. They expressed concerns about their course grade when it could be affected by the work of others. For some, the opportunity to provide constructive feedback to their peers and use strategies of conflict resolution was also new and challenging. In general, graduate students were comfortable with the amount of preparation and number of group activities that are an integral part of TBL. Concerns about fairness in grading, however, needed to be explicitly addressed by the instructors. Tools were developed to "measure" each student's participation in small group discussions and assignments. Both undergraduate and graduate students needed guidance from instructors in managing their concerns about grading as well as how to respectfully manage disparate opinions.

Students have consistently reported that they need more time to maximize SCALE-UP classroom learning experiences. In our graduate course, students requested more time to explore health policy issues, discuss varied solutions, and exchange ideas and experiences in both small and large groups. While undergraduate students would also benefit from longer class sessions in the SCALE-UP classroom, we currently cannot resolve this issue with our space limitations and scheduling conflicts with their clinical experiences. However, the move to new space will provide us with more flexibility, with high-capacity SCALE-UP classrooms and less competition for classroom space.

Faculty must develop new teaching skills such as team building, group facilitation, and fielding complex questions from students "on-the-fly." Group management and grading strategies are common challenges. We need to grow comfortable with less control over what happens in the classroom, and teaching in the midst of students, rather than in front of them.

NEW DIRECTIONS FOR TEACHING AND LEARNING • DOI: 10.1002/tl

Mutual support, discussion of challenges, and group problem solving is just as important for faculty as for students. Throughout this project, faculty and staff have benefitted from discussions of experiences and from ongoing development opportunities and collaboration. Articles and teaching tools as well as examples of syllabi, assignments, and classroom management strategies used in other SCALE-UP classroom courses have been helpful for faculty making new changes. These types of resources have been available for our faculty through our online SCALE-UP classroom site (see Table 9.1).

Finally, an important lesson has been seeing that these new approaches have enhanced our faculty members' interest in discovering teaching methods that facilitate both student and faculty engagement and improve learning outcomes. Research has consistently demonstrated that the use of specific educational approaches is less important than the extent to which students are engaged in a collaborative learning process with their professors (Smith et al. 2005). We have challenged ourselves to avoid dichotomizing teaching to either lecture or active learning, and have instead focused on how we can work with students to discover which pedagogies are most effective to improve student outcomes. Our experiences with the implementation of the SCALE-UP classroom have led us to expand our methods of teaching and promoted a willingness to take risks to improve our learning environments. In the future, we anticipate expanding our research of student engagement to delineate how classroom environments and pedagogies may impact learning gains.

References

Beichner, R., J. Saul, D. S. Abbott, J. J. Morse, D. L. Deardorff, R. J. Allain, S. Bonham, M. Dancy, and J. Risley. 2007. "Student Centered Activities for Large Enrollment Undergraduate Programs (SCALE-UP) Project." In *Research-Based Reform in University Physics*, edited by E. F. Redish and P. J. Cooney, 1–42. College Park, MD: American Association of Physics Teachers.

Benner, P., M. Sutphen, V. Leonard, and L. Day. 2009. *Educating Nurses: A Call for Radical Transformation*. San Francisco, CA: Jossey-Bass.

Garrison, D. R., and N. D. Vaughan. 2008. *Blended Learning in Higher Education: Framework, Principles, and Guidelines*. San Francisco, CA: Jossey-Bass.

Michaelsen, L., and M. Sweet. 2011. "Team-Based Learning." In *Evidence-Based Teaching*, New Directions for Teaching and Learning, no. 128, edited by W. Buskist and J. E. Groccia, 41–51. San Francisco, CA: Jossey-Bass.

Smith, K. A., S. D. Sheppard, D. W. Johnson, and R. T. Johnson. 2005. "Pedagogies of Engagement: Classroom-Based Practices." *Journal of Engineering Education*, 94 (1): 87–101.

BETH FAHLBERG is a clinical associate professor in the School of Nursing at the University of Wisconsin-Madison.

ELIZABETH RICE, PhD, PMHNP-BC, is a clinical associate professor and the director of the Doctor of Nursing Practice Program in the University of Wisconsin School of Nursing.

REBECCA MUEHRER is an assistant professor in the School of Nursing at the University of Wisconsin-Madison.

DANIELLE BREY obtained a BS in Sociology from the University of Wisconsin-La Crosse and is currently a graduate student in the School of Social Work at the University of Wisconsin-Madison.

NEW DIRECTIONS FOR TEACHING AND LEARNING • DOI: 10.1002/tl

10

This concluding chapter helps us look toward the future of active learning spaces as they enter the mainstream.

Conclusion: Advancing Active Learning Spaces

Aimee L. Whiteside

As we conclude this *Active Learning Spaces* volume, it is clear, in some ways, that we've come a long way from EDUCAUSE's foundational work, *Learning Spaces* (Oblinger 2006). This new compilation of essays highlights innovations in research, pedagogy, student learning, and faculty development for active learning spaces.

D. Christopher Brooks, J. D. Walker, and Paul Baepler (Editors' Notes) expertly frame the volume by introducing us to how physical space "constrains and/or facilitates the manner in which individuals relate to or experience a space" (3). From a helpful exploration of physical space in general, they connect us to physical space for student learning and then update us on the significant advances in the literature. Finally, they remind us of breakthrough initiatives that set the field in motion, such as MIT's TEAL, NC-State's SCALE-UP, and the University of Minnesota's active learning classrooms (ALCs).

This volume demonstrates that we are making considerable advances within active learning spaces. In each chapter, we are introduced to a research-based exploration of an active learning space (for example, ALCs, TILE, and Collaborative Café). The chapters and the studies they cite present strong evidence that active learning spaces improve student satisfaction as well as learning outcomes (Brooks 2011, 2012; Brooks and Solheim Chapter 5 of this volume; Langley and Guzey Chapter 7; Van Horne et al. Chapter 2; Walker, Brooks, and Baepler 2011; Whiteside, Brooks, and Walker 2010). We are inspired by these research-based explorations and by such engaged professionals and their willing students. In sum, it seems that we are ready for the next phase of active learning spaces: one where these spaces emerge into the mainstream.

So, how can we continue our essential research, yet also begin to move to something more scalable? It is a difficult question to answer, predominantly because the average traditional classroom has not been updated for

NEW DIRECTIONS FOR TEACHING AND LEARNING, no. 137, Spring 2014 © 2014 Wiley Periodicals, Inc.
Published online in Wiley Online Library (wileyonlinelibrary.com) • DOI: 10.1002/tl.20090

decades. Editors Brooks, Walker, and Baepler assert that many of our classrooms still embody a 20th century framework. True, the vast majority of our higher education physical classroom spaces have kept to a similar appearance for the past 20–30 years. Sadly, active learning spaces represent only a very small percentage of our nation's higher education classrooms.

Moreover, the editors contend that our physical classroom spaces have not caught up with digitally enhanced pedagogies. With extraordinary technological advances emerging just within the past five years, how have the majority of our physical classrooms not kept pace with the changing times as well as instructors' and students' growing needs? Certainly, there are a whole host of reasons why traditional classrooms have not kept pace and why active learning spaces are not peppered across our higher education campuses, including sheer cost, the change-resistant elements, multiple needs for one space, and the time- and support-intensive demands for online and blended learning. Given these challenges and obstacles, how do we advance active learning spaces? In short, we read and lead; we keep researching; and we continually update our administrators regarding the immense educational value of active learning spaces.

Read and Lead

As educational researchers and specialists, it is important to showcase our leadership through a vast knowledge of literature, by keeping up on advances in our network of colleagues, and through a strong focus on pedagogy and student learning. Present your research at conferences and other events and, most importantly, network and learn from other educators, faculty development specialists, and educational researchers. Partner with them. Learn about active learning space initiatives on the horizon at schools around the globe. Also, share, validate, and improve upon each other's research instruments.

Additionally, lead by focusing on student learning, pedagogy, and active learning spaces. Try not to get duped into the latest trends that "threaten" higher education, such as MOOCs and what John Sener (2012) calls the "cyberdystopia" of the American Educational System. In truth, although online offerings are still on the rise, online education, as a whole, has recently experienced a slowing in its overall growth (Lederman 2013). Likewise, a recent Bill and Melinda Gates Foundation research project suggests that most community college students overwhelmingly prefer to take classes face-to-face over online courses (Jaggars Smith 2013). One might hypothesize that undergraduate students may also have these same face-to-face preferences and, perhaps, to an even greater extent (Dahlstrom, Dziuban, and Walker 2013). As such, we must be prepared to meet student demand for face-to-face classrooms and to provide active learning spaces that enhance student learning experiences.

NEW DIRECTIONS FOR TEACHING AND LEARNING • DOI: 10.1002/tl

Keep Researching

Effective research begins by involving a wide variety of stakeholders to help us ask, answer, and prioritize important research questions for active learning spaces. This research plays a pivotal role in building a persuasive case for active learning spaces, and there has been a considerable amount of research that provides clear evidence of improved student learning in these spaces (Brooks 2011, 2012; Brooks and Solheim Chapter 5 of this volume; Langley and Guzey Chapter 7; Van Horne et al. Chapter 2; Walker, Brooks, and Baepler 2011; Whiteside, Brooks, and Walker 2010).

An important next step involves developing a research plan that meets the needs of all of our stakeholders. Brooks and Solheim (Chapter 5) lay out an exceptional research agenda for active learning spaces. They suggest five areas of continued research, including (1) replicating previous quasi-experimental designs, (2) addressing "cross-disciplinary and cross-institutional perspectives," (3) comparing active learning pedagogies, (4) understanding which specific features yield more results, and (5) examining ALCs in regard to demographic characteristics (60).

As you plan your research agenda, strive for mixed-methods studies with a careful mix of qualitative and quantitative research strategies. While administrators and key stakeholders demand statistics, they are often most compelled by rich, powerful instructor and student narratives. Be vigilant in your data planning and data collection processes. Be ruthless about collecting pre-post data, including photos of the space(s) and instructor and student interviews, focus groups, and surveys. You cannot go back in time, so plan accordingly and opt for more rather than less data. Finally, write up a one-page, easy-to-scan synopsis of your active learning spaces research results for busy administrators.

Update Administrators

Finally, make a rhetorically compelling case for active learning spaces to present to upper administrators and key stakeholders. Show that you know the literature and, more importantly, that you can quickly synthesize it. Discuss and showcase the powerful partnerships you created, including the faculty development and support infrastructure (Jorn, Whiteside, and Duin 2009). Finally, as mentioned earlier, provide short, clear, and scannable one-page synopses of the research and, when possible, relate the results directly to student retention, student learning outcomes, and/or assessments that are directly aligned with accrediting agencies as well as with university, college, departmental, and programmatic goals. Overall, be ready to easily articulate and demonstrate the research-based need for active learning spaces.

In sum, the past decade of research in active learning spaces progressed immensely as showcased in this volume. That said, it is essential that we keep advocating for active learning spaces by keeping current on the literature, by nurturing and refining our faculty development and support, by creating powerful, strategic partnerships, by continuing our strategic research, and by experimenting with the crucial harmonizing pedagogies for more effective student learning. With our leadership and vision in the coming decade, active learning spaces may emerge as the new normal that transforms the traditional landscape of face-to-face teaching and learning experiences.

References

Brooks, D. C. 2011. "Space Matters: The Impact of Formal Learning Environments on Student Learning." *British Journal of Educational Technology* 42 (5): 719–726.
Brooks, D. C. 2012. "Space and Consequences: The Impact of Different Formal Learning Spaces on Instructor and Student Behavior." *Journal of Learning Spaces* 1 (2). http://z.umn.edu/jols.
Dahlstrom, E., C. Dziuban, and J. D. Walker. 2013. "ECAR Study of Undergraduate Students and Information Technology, 2013" (Research Report). Louisville, CO: EDUCAUSE Center for Analysis and Research. https://net.educause.edu/ir/library/pdf/ERS1302/ERS1302.pdf.
Jaggars Smith, S. 2013. *Choosing Between Online and Face-to-Face Courses: Community College Student Voices.* Community College Research Center. New York, NY: Columbia University.
Jorn, L. A., A. L. Whiteside, and A. H. Duin. 2009. "PAIR-Up." *EDUCAUSE Review* 44: 12–15.
Lederman, D. 2013. "Growth for Online Learning." *Inside Higher Ed.* http://www.insidehighered.com/news/2013/01/08/survey-finds-online-enrollments-slow-continue-grow#.UhY0ZbxnCBB.
Oblinger, D. G. (Ed.). 2006. *Learning Spaces.* Boulder, CO: EDUCAUSE. http://www.educause.edu/research-and-publications/books/learning-spaces.
Sener, J. 2012. *The Seven Futures of American Education: Improving Learning and Teaching in a Screen-Captured World.* North Charleston, SC: CreateSpace.
Walker, J. D., D. C. Brooks, and P. Baepler. 2011. "Pedagogy and Space: Empirical Research in New Learning Environments." *EDUCAUSE Quarterly* 34 (4). http://z.umn.edu/eq1.
Whiteside, A. L., D. C. Brooks, and J. D. Walker. 2010. "Making the Case for Space: Three Years of Empirical Research on Learning Environments." *EDUCAUSE Quarterly* 33 (3). http://z.umn.edu/22m.

AIMEE L. WHITESIDE is an assistant professor in the English and Writing Department at the University of Tampa.

INDEX

Abbott, D. S., 1, 18, 27, 33–35, 86
Active learning, 12–16; in labs, 12–13; in lectures, 13–14; in studios, 14–16; technology in, 9–11
Active learning classroom (ALC), 1; challenges of, 63–70; and educational alliances, 27–39; future of, 15–16; introductory biology course in, 71–76; in nursing education, 85–93; and pedagogy, 53–60; quasi-experimental designs to assess, 4–5; at University of Minnesota, 1, 95; vs. traditional classrooms, 63–64
Active learning spaces, advancing, 95–98; continuation of research work, 97; leadership and learning in, 96; overview, 95–96; updating of administrators in, 97–98
Adams, P., 3
ALC. See Active learning classroom (ALC)
Allain, R. J., 1, 18, 27, 86
Amedeo, D., 2, 5, 6, 27
Andrews, V., 3
Arthur, I. T., 41, 51
Astin, A., 15
Atlay, M., 3
"Auditoria," 11

Baepler, P., 3, 4, 8, 27, 29, 40, 53, 54, 63, 95, 97
Beichner, B., 79
Beichner, R. J., 1, 3, 9, 16, 18, 27, 78, 86
Being wrong, 37
"Beholding area," 11
Belcher, J., 1, 3, 27
Benner, P., 85
Bentham, J., 38
Besette, M., 3
Beyer, C. H., 75
Bill and Melinda Gates Foundation, 96
Billson, J. M., 28, 32, 38
Blaich, C., 76
Bligh, B., 3
Boddington, A., 3
Bonham, S., 18, 86
Bordin, E. S., 28

Boys, J., 3
Bransford, J. D., 29
Brey, D., 85, 94
Brooks, D. C., 1, 4, 5, 8, 18, 27, 29, 53, 54, 61, 63, 71, 95, 97
Brown, A. L., 29
Bruff, D., 83

Center for Innovative Teaching and Learning (CITL), 49
Center for Teaching (CfT), 78, 79, 83
CfT. See Center for Teaching (CfT)
CfT staff, 79
Challenges, active learning classrooms and, 63–70; absence of focal point in, 64–65; absence of instructor as focal point, 66–68; addressing challenges, 69–70; challenges imposed by changes in teaching roles, 66–69; challenges imposed by physical layout of, 64–66; loss of wider community in, 68–69; multiple distractions in, 65–66; overwhelming technology in, 66
Chickering, A. W., 28, 29, 33
CITL. See Center for Innovative Teaching and Learning (CITL)
Classroom relationships. See Educational alliances
Cocking, R. R., 29
Cole, R., 84
Collaboration Café, 41–50; conducive space to collaboration, 44–45; design of room and furniture in, 45–47; instrument and data collection for, 43–44; key findings of research, 44–49; overall comfort in, 47; overview, 41; research methods to study, 41–44; results and key points from studies, 49–50; technology usage in, 47–49
Cooperation, in ALC, 35–36; cooperative teaching-learning practices, 35; student bonding and support, 36
Cooperative teaching-learning practices, 35–36
Cotner, S., 53, 54, 71
Creswell, J. W., 19, 43

Dahlstrom, E., 96
Dancy, M., 18, 86
Danziger, M., 3
Day, L., 85
Deardorff, D. L., 1, 18, 27, 86
DEO. *See* Departmental Executive Officers (DEO)
Departmental Executive Officers (DEO), 80–82
Difference-of-Means Tests, 57–58; for aggregated student grades, 57; for grades on comparable student assignments, 57–58
Diluting passivity, in ALC, 33
Dori, Y. J., 1, 3, 27
Duin, A. H., 3, 97
Dziuban, C., 96

Educational alliances, 27–39; cooperation, 35–36; data for, 29; effective communication and feedback, 33–35; findings of research on, 29–38; key features of, 28; mutual respect, 29–31; overview, 27–28; research methods for, 28–29; shared responsibility for learning, 31–33; trust and security, 36–38
EDUCAUSE, 1, 95
Effective communication, in ALC, 33–35; higher quality of, 34–35; new avenues for, 33; technology and physical features in, 34
Egalitarianism, 31
Endo, J. J., 28
Equivalency tests, for demographic variables, 56

Faculty Learning Community (FLC), 49
Fahlberg, B., 85, 93
Family Social Science (FSoS), 54
Feedback mechanism, in ALC, 33–35
Fink, L. D., 55, 76
FLC. *See* Faculty Learning Community (FLC)
"Flipped classroom," 16
Florman, J. C., 17, 26, 77, 84
FSoS. *See* Family Social Science (FSoS)

Gaffney, J., 79
Gallimore, R., 43

Gamson, Z. F., 28, 29, 33
Garrison, D. R., 90
Gateway Science Workshop Program, 76
Gillmore, G. M., 75
Golledge, R. G., 2, 5, 6, 27
Gorman, K. S., 63, 70
Guzey, S. S., 71, 76, 95, 97

Hake, R., 12
Handelsman, J., 71
Harpel, R. L., 28
Hartley, J., 71
Henderson, A., 43
Hiebert, J., 43
Hill, C. E., 39
Holeton, R., 3
How College Affects Students, 30
How People Learn, 29
Hult, E., 3
Hunley, S., 3

ILD. *See* Interactive lecture demo (ILD)
IMDB, 10
Information Technology Services-Instructional Services (ITS-IS), 78, 83
Ingram, B. F., 17, 26
Interactive lecture demo (ILD), 13
Introductory biology course, in ALC, 71–76; conventional resources for, 74; insights of, 75; overview, 71–72; pedagogical practices in, 73–75; qualitative case study on, 72–75; team teaching in, 74
ITS-IS. *See* Information Technology Services-Instructional Services (ITS-IS)
ITS-IS staff, 79

Jaggars Smith, S., 96
Jankowska, M., 3
Jesse, M., 17, 25
Johnson, B., 43
Johnson, D. W., 35, 68, 78, 93
Johnson, R. T., 35, 68, 78, 93
Jordan, B., 43
Jorn, L. A., 1, 97
Journal of Learning Spaces, 1

Knight, A. B., 55
Kuh, G., 77, 83

OTHER TITLES AVAILABLE IN THE
NEW DIRECTIONS FOR TEACHING AND LEARNING SERIES
Catherine M. Wehlburg, Editor-in-Chief
R. Eugene Rice, Consulting Editor

For a complete list of back issues, please visit www.josseybass.com/go/ndtl

TL136   ***Doing the Scholarship of Teaching and Learning: Measuring Systematic Changes to Teaching and Improvements in Learning***
Regan A. R. Gurung, Janie H. Wilson, Editors
The Scholarship of Teaching and Learning (SoTL) should be an integral part of every academic's life, representing not only the pinnacle of effortful teaching, but also standing side by side with more conventional disciplinary scholarship. Although practiced by many instructors for years, SoTL has garnered national attention resulting in a spate of new journals to publish pedagogical research. SoTL helps students, fosters faculty development, and has been integrated into higher education in *Scholarship of Teaching and Learning Reconsidered* (Hutchings, Huber, & Ciccone, 2011). This volume provides readers with challenges that will motivate them to engage in SoTL and take their pedagogical research further. We include many key features aimed to help both the teacher new to research and SoTL and also researchers who may have a long list of scholarly publications in non-pedagogical areas and who have not conducted research.
ISBN 978-11188-38679

TL135   ***From Entitlement to Engagement: Affirming Millennial Students' Egos in the Higher Education Classroom***
Dave S. Knowlton, Kevin Jack Hagopian, Editors
This volume of New Directions for Teaching and Learning addresses theories and practices surrounding the entitled, self-absorbed students called Millennials. Stereotypical Millennials are often addicted to gadgets, demand service more than education, and hold narrow perspectives about themselves and those around them; when seen through this lens, Millennial students can understandably frustrate the most dedicated of professors.
   The contributors to this volume show how new and better educational outcomes can emerge if professors reconsider Millennials. First and foremost, many of these students simply don't fit their stereotype. Beyond that, the authors urge faculty to question commonly held assumptions, showing them how to reevaluate their pedagogical practices, relationships with students, and the norms of college classrooms. Contributors focus on practical means to achieve new and more evocative outcomes by treating Millennial students as serious collaborators in the learning process, thereby helping those students to more closely identify with their own education. The assignments that professors give, the treatment of topics that they broach, and the digital tools that they ask students to employ can shift students' concerns away from a narrow focus on impersonal, technical mastery of content and toward seeing themselves as Millennial thinkers who fuse their lives with their learning.
ISBN 978-11187-70108

NEW DIRECTIONS FOR TEACHING AND LEARNING

ORDER FORM SUBSCRIPTION AND SINGLE ISSUES

DISCOUNTED BACK ISSUES:

Use this form to receive 20% off all back issues of *New Directions for Teaching and Learning*.
All single issues priced at **$23.20** (normally $29.00)

TITLE	ISSUE NO.	ISBN

Call 888-378-2537 or see mailing instructions below. When calling, mention the promotional code JBNND to receive your discount. For a complete list of issues, please visit www.josseybass.com/go/ndtl

SUBSCRIPTIONS: (1 YEAR, 4 ISSUES)

☐ New Order   ☐ Renewal

U.S.	☐ Individual: $89	☐ Institutional: $311
CANADA/MEXICO	☐ Individual: $89	☐ Institutional: $351
ALL OTHERS	☐ Individual: $113	☐ Institutional: $385

Call 888-378-2537 or see mailing and pricing instructions below.
Online subscriptions are available at www.onlinelibrary.wiley.com

ORDER TOTALS:

Issue / Subscription Amount: $ _____

Shipping Amount: $ _____
(for single issues only – subscription prices include shipping)

Total Amount: $ _____

SHIPPING CHARGES:	
First Item	$6.00
Each Add'l Item	$2.00

(No sales tax for U.S. subscriptions. Canadian residents, add GST for subscription orders. Individual rate subscriptions must be paid by personal check or credit card. Individual rate subscriptions may not be resold as library copies.)

BILLING & SHIPPING INFORMATION:

☐ **PAYMENT ENCLOSED:** *(U.S. check or money order only. All payments must be in U.S. dollars.)*

☐ **CREDIT CARD:** ☐ VISA ☐ MC ☐ AMEX

Card number _____ Exp. Date_____

Card Holder Name_____ Card Issue # _____

Signature _____ Day Phone _____

☐ **BILL ME:** *(U.S. institutional orders only. Purchase order required.)*

Purchase order # _____
Federal Tax ID 13559302 • GST 89102-8052

Name_____

Address_____

Phone_____ E-mail_____

Copy or detach page and send to: **John Wiley & Sons, One Montgomery Street, Suite 1200, San Francisco, CA 94104-4594**

Order Form can also be faxed to: **888-481-2665**

PROMO JBNND

Great Resources for Higher Education Professionals

Student Affairs Today
12 issues for $225 (print) / $180 (e)

Get innovative best practices for student affairs plus lawsuit summaries to keep your institution out of legal trouble. It's packed with advice on offering effective services, assessing and funding programs, and meeting legal requirements.

studentaffairstodaynewsletter.com

Campus Legal Advisor
12 issues for $210 (print) / $170 (e)

From complying with the ADA and keeping residence halls safe to protecting the privacy of student information, this monthly publication delivers proven strategies to address the tough legal issues you face on campus.

campuslegaladvisor.com

Campus Security Report
12 issues for $210 (print) / $170 (e)

A publication that helps you effectively manage the challenges in keeping your campus, students, and employees safe. From protecting students on campus after dark to interpreting the latest laws and regulations, *Campus Security Report* has answers you need.

campussecurityreport.com

National Teaching & Learning Forum
6 issues for $65 (print or e)

From big concepts to practical details and from cutting-edge techniques to established wisdom, NTLF is your resource for cross-disciplinary discourse on student learning. With it, you'll gain insights into learning theory, classroom management, lesson planning, scholarly publishing, team teaching, online learning, pedagogical innovation, technology, and more.

ntlf.com

Disability Compliance for Higher Education
12 issues for $230 (print) / $185 (e)

This publication combines interpretation of disability laws with practical implementation strategies to help you accommodate students and staff with disabilities. It offers data collection strategies, intervention models for difficult students, service review techniques, and more.

disabilitycomplianceforhighereducation.com

Dean & Provost
12 issues for $225 (print) / $180 (e)

From budgeting to faculty tenure and from distance learning to labor relations, *Dean & Provost* gives you innovative ways to manage the challenges of leading your institution. Learn how to best use limited resources, safeguard your institution from frivolous lawsuits, and more.

deanandprovost.com

Enrollment Management Report
12 issues for $230 (print) / $185 (e)

Find out which enrollment strategies are working for your colleagues, which aren't, and why. This publication gives you practical guidance on all aspects—including records, registration, recruitment, orientation, admissions, retention, and more.

enrollmentmanagementreport.com

WANT TO SUBSCRIBE?
Go online or call: 888.378.2537.

JB JOSSEY-BASS
A Wiley Brand

Great Resources for Higher Education Professionals

College Athletics and the Law

12 issues for $225 (print) / $180 (e)

Develop a legally sound "game plan" for your institution's athletic programs! Each month, you get expert coaching on how to meet NCAA and Title IX requirements, negotiate coaching contracts, support athletes with disabilities, and more.

collegeathleticslaw.com

FERPA Answer Book and Bulletin

6 issues for $220 (print only)

Includes a full binder with all you need to know about FERPA

From safekeeping students' education records to learning how you can share personal information, this is your professional survival guide. It includes the latest changes to the regs, how to comply, and newly issued FPCO policy letters, administrative and judicial decisions, and more.

About Campus

6 issues for $65 (print only)

An exciting and eclectic mix of articles — designed to illuminate the critical issues faced by both student affairs and academic affairs as they work on their shared goal: to help students learn. Topics include promoting student learning, meeting the needs of a diverse student population, assessing student learning, and accommodating the changing student culture.

Assessment Update

6 issues for $135 (print) / $110 (e)

Get the latest assessment techniques for higher education. *Assessment Update* is your resource for evaluating learning communities, performance indicators, assessing student engagement, using electronic portfolios, new assessment approaches and more.

assessmentupdate.com

Recruiting & Retaining Adult Learners

12 issues for $225 (print) / $180 (e)

This publication addresses the challenges and opportunities you face in recruiting, retaining, and educating your adult students. Find strategies to target your orientation to adult learners, encourage adult-friendly support systems, take advantage of new technologies, and more.

recruitingretainingadultlearners.com

The Successful Registrar

12 issues for $230 (print) / $185 (e)

Get practical guidance on all aspects of your job—from implementing the newest technology and successful registration programs to complying with FERPA, and from training your staff and student workers to security issues and transcript management.

thesuccessfulregistrar.com

The Department Chair

4 issues for $99 (print) / $89 (e)

From retaining your best faculty and resolving conflict to measuring learning and implementing new policies, this resource arms you with the practical information you need to manage your department effectively.

departmentchairs.org/journal.aspx

WANT TO SUBSCRIBE?

Go online or call: 888.378.2537.

JB JOSSEY-BASS™
A Wiley Brand